THE HAPPY CLOSET

Well-Being is Well-Dressed

THE HAPPY CLOSET

CLOSET

Well-Being is Well-Dressed

Annmarie O'Connor

Gill Books

Gill Books
Hume Avenue
Park West
Dublin 12
www.gillbooks.ie

© Annmarie O'Connor 2016

978 07171 6918 4

Designed and print origination by O'K Graphic Design, Dublin
Printed by ScandBook AB, Sweden

This book is typeset in 11/17 pt Minion
Chapter headings in Advert Light

*The paper used in this book comes from the wood pulp of managed forests. For
every tree felled, at least one tree is planted, thereby renewing natural resources.*

A CIP catalogue record for this book is available from the British Library.
5 4 3 2 1

To women everywhere. Find the space to be yourself.

Acknowledgements

I'd like to acknowledge everyone who has made *The Happy Closet* a reality. Thank you to the team at Gill for their sterling support. Thank you to my family, friends, colleagues and readers. Thank you to every woman who has opened her closet doors to me. My heartfelt gratitude to you all.

CONTENTS

INTRODUCTION

My name is Annmarie O'Connor. I'm a fashion journalist and stylist by trade. I'm also a reformed hoarder by habit. That's why I've written this book.

For years, I lived with the ironic dilemma of having a wardobe full of clothes and nothing to wear. Much like a magpie, my brain seemed wired towards amassing the shiny and showy, with little regard for how it fit into my lifestyle. Despite endless vows to downsize, I found myself waving at the shadow of a groundhog weighed down in turbans and kaftans screaming that he didn't have the right shoes (vermin can be real divas).

Dressing became a chore, not least due to the vast volume of clothing I had accumulated. Sure, my closet was colourful (so is an acid trip), but it lacked synergy and flow. The only thread keeping it all together was the question 'Why?', which, if tugged at even slightly, would cause a drag-queen pile-up of sequins, glitter and studs. So I kept a wide berth of that frayed emotional hem, donned my military epaulettes and soldiered on.

That's the thing about hoarding. It's by nature self-perpetuating and rarely results in a cull. In fact, any decluttering I attempted just served to reinforce the prospect of loss and emotional vulnerability, which led me to procrastinate and over-rationalise why I 'needed' so much. Until I got real.

What started as a simple act of tidying soon exposed a full-length mirror of emotional triggers. Like any clearing exercise, things had to get messier before they got better. Not only did the process shed a harsh glare on the person I was pretending to be (hot-shot influencer), but the naked bulb hanging over my shopping habits wasn't exactly flattering (shabby impostor). I was a classic impulse buyer and I had the receipts to prove it – lots of them. Once I got clear about my personal pitfalls (the need to impress, the desire to be accepted), I was better positioned to confront my inner hoarder and reframe the persistent patterns that were creating war within my wardrobe.

This epiphany did more than just declutter my closet; it inspired me to create a system to identify the emotional hang-ups and habits that underpin our closet happiness. This is what I'm here to share with you – the secret to achieving closet zen. By combining mindfulness exercises with awareness therapy, *The Happy Closet* aims to help release the unconscious inclinations behind the nine core closet types: Impulse Buyer, Secret Shopper, Doomsday Prepper, Tired & Emotional, Black Widow, Split Personality, Martyr Mom, Sale Sniper and Perfect 9. By figuring out which you are, you'll discover how to overcome your personal trip-wires, reframe shopping patterns and, more important, dress the person you are – *today.*

Let's be clear: this isn't a run-of-the-mill wardrobe clear-out. It's about sifting beneath the layers of confusion and finding out what's really driving our collective primal impulses – that hunter-gatherer DNA that insists on colonising every square inch of space. It's only in understanding what makes us tick that we can evolve from collecting to curating. Let the inside match the outside and watch the magic happen. If you've ever wanted to have more with less, then it's time to discover how happy your closet can be.

CHAPTER ONE

OPENING THE DOORS

THE BIG REVEAL

'If you can't get rid of the skeleton in your closet, you'd best take it out and teach it to dance.'

GEORGE BERNARD SHAW

How do you feel when you open your closet? More to the point, how does your closet feel? Buried beneath those forgettable fads, questionable trends and 'oh dear, what was I thinking?' is a pile of useless emotional baggage. Bet you didn't see it. Well, guess what? You're not alone. Your closet is more than just a collection of clothes. It's a deeply vulnerable space containing layers of old energy, which, when coupled with an evolutionary gathering instinct, can create chaos. And let's face it: a chaotic closet is not a happy closet.

That's where I come in. Call it a closet intervention, but I'm here to help you confront your inner hoarder and address the behaviours that have led to your not-so-uncommon case of sartorial overwhelm.

Granted, mindfulness and fashion aren't the most obvious twosome: one commits to the soul's urge while the other commits to a pair of Charlotte Olympia calf-hair wedges when the rent is due. That said, their paradoxical pairing can help even the most seasoned stockpiler distinguish between keepsakes and keeping something for the sake of it.

Old attachments, a fear of change, regret and compulsion are the most common psychological blocks that keep us locked into repetitive routines, such as how we shop and why we hoard. In fact, our habits are so unconscious, they tend to happen without our permission.

You can blame it on the basal ganglia – a group of cells in the brain that dates back to our cave-people days. Responsible for forming and storing habits, these little fellas act much like a zip file in that they help our brain's hard drive function more efficiently. Once we've mastered a habit ,be it walking or driving (or shopping), it becomes ingrained or 'automatic' so that our minds are free to focus on other more immediate concerns.

A bit of bad news: habits never disappear. Ever. What's more, the brain can't distinguish between a good and a bad one. In other words, your penchant for green tea and your love of designer T-shirts receive equal billing. Those basal ganglia are non-denominational, equal-opportunities employers, bless them.

All it takes is a trigger to access the habit from our memory – which explains why we drove to the shopping centre instead of our mother's after work last Thursday (late-night shopping, anyone?) and why even the sight of a shoe sale requires blinkers and/or heavy sedation.

Over time and with repetition, habits detonate with even the smallest persuasion and, in turn, disable our ability to make careful and considered choices. Before you know it, you've fallen down the rabbit hole, taken advice from a caterpillar smoking a hookah and are experiencing one hell of an identity crisis. You can blame it on some questionable tea or you can get your butt out of wonderland before you totally lose your head.

Feeling a bit exposed? Of course. Closets are the seat of our deepest, darkest shopping secrets. By opening the doors, you are effectively revealing your biggest weaknesses and the state of your self-esteem at a given moment. Is everything folded, orderly, neat? Hidden in boxes with the tags still intact? Balled in a corner, mismanaged, badly in need of repair? Or are you operating more of a floordrobe-style operation – bags of swag strewn carelessly in a Lindsay Lohan-meets-Tracey Emin homage?

Before launching into ambush mode, it's time to get an insight into your closet personality – the hidden behaviour that got you here in the first place. Read on to find the nine closet types, each with their own traits to help you identify the common tics feeding your inner pack rat. It's only by identifying these hang-ups that we can successfully modify the pesky practices that have your closet in a pickle.

Grab a cup of tea, a comfy chair and prepare to get honest. Trust me, this is the easy part. Once you've admitted to going off the rails, that's when you can start cleaning up your act – one skeleton at a time. Bye-bye dread and indecision; hello thoughtful dresser. Prepare for some straight talking. Every closet has a story to tell. It's time to discover what yours has to say about you.

THE NINE CLOSET TYPES

'There are women in my closet, hanging on the hangers – a different woman for each suit, each dress, each pair of shoes.'

MARYA HORNBACHER

Impulse Buyer

Impulse Buyer is an emotional creature. Socially driven and highly image-conscious, she is more inclined to resort to retail therapy than Facebook for a status update. Shopping is strictly a hedonistic pleasure: often spontaneous, never planned and with little regard for the consequences. That would explain Impulse Buyer's closet: a hot-bed of conflict where belligerent occupation by half-baked trends has supplanted time-honoured basics.

Much like a commercial radio station, Impulse Buyer has a set of clothes on heavy rotation, despite having a huge back catalogue. One of the most random things in her wardrobe is a pair of simple black trousers that look desperately out of place among the studded shoulder pads and sequin hotpants, not to mention that fringed Day-Glo leather jacket which she once spotted on Cher at Caesar's Palace. Cue buying frenzy …

Her recurring online shopping habit, which she blames squarely on a combination of wine and Wi-Fi, doesn't help matters much. But those crystal-embellished Christian Louboutin ballet flats might actually survive more than two wears, thus validating her €745 splurge … *she hopes.* Aspiring to a look modelled by a 16-year old Brazilian waif has its own set of issues – especially when she discovers (not so shockingly) that a bandage dress looks a tad different wedged over a pair of 36DD boobs. And yet she hoards, convinced one day her curves might comply.

From time to time, she'll open the wardrobe and panic that her motley clothing crew might make a break for freedom and smother her during the night. But this does little to dissuade the Impulse Buyer, who keeps a mental lock on the closet door until buyer's remorse becomes too much and a massive cull ensues. With that, everything that isn't nailed down or zipped onto her body is dumped into black bags. Of course, all this does is make space for new clothes to collect.

Secret Shopper

Secret Shopper doesn't believe in sharing. Like an MI6 agent, the Secret Shopper intelligence operation is purely clandestine. She doesn't like witnesses, especially when it comes to how much she spends. Shopping is done alone and with separate credit cards, online parcels are sent to a PO box and all references to newly acquired purchases remain highly encrypted.

To avoid interception, Secret Shopper stashes that feather-trimmed leotard in a labyrinth closet so stealthily arranged it risks never being found. When she does remember to retrieve it (if she can find it), her back-story is legit. No one can argue with the fact that she bought it ages ago – especially not her husband. That's how she likes it.

There really is no need for him to know how much she shops. Come to think of it, *she* doesn't even know how much she shops! Some would consider that a bad thing, but she likes to think ignorance is bliss. There is a reason she keeps everything under wraps, of course. A lot of her clothes haven't even been worn and people just can't understand why she continues to buy when she already has so much.

So her stashing technique serves her well – except the last time Secret Shopper took a good look at her closet, it was like seeing things for the first time. She does cringe at having forgotten about that Carmen Miranda dress with the life-size pineapple appliqués, but that doesn't change the fact that she still intends wearing it … one day. Should her cover be blown (along with her budget), she keeps those swing tags intact and receipts at the ready for a swift emergency exit. Hey, it's all part of the job.

Doomsday Prepper

Doomsday Prepper is the original stockpiler. Operating on a well-honed survivalist instinct, she believes in being prepared for any and all wardrobe emergencies. Statements like 'I need it', 'I definitely need it', 'It could come in handy' and 'You never know' have led Doomsday Prepper to infiltrate every square inch of space in her house.

Her husband shares one wardobe with her two youngest kids, which leaves her with the other three – not including the hall closet … and the closet in the spare room … and the shed. Then there's the purpose-built walk-in wardrobe that could double as a potential air raid shelter. Her mantra is 'You can never be too prepared'. Self-sufficiency, after all, is key to surviving the world of fashion, which means storing anything that may, might, could or would be of use at no specific time in the future.

According to Doomsday, cosmic spite demands that the very instant you part with that Isabel Marant prairie dress, you'll need to wear it. Then what? It's not that she's an extremist, you know; she just likes to think of herself as ready for any fashion emergency.

On average, she wears about 20% of her wardrobe, with the other 80% saving her from a massive meltdown. The prospect of loss (and looking like a hungry dystopian teen from a post-apocalyptic blockbuster) is just too catastrophic to bear and thus she continues to collect rather than select.

Sure, getting dressed can be a bit painstaking with all the boxes, over-stuffed rails and the occasional missing pet, but it's worth the peace of mind.

Tired & Emotional

Tired & Emotional is the proud owner of a love-worn wardrobe. Although not exactly vintage, the heartfelt narrative behind each and every moth-eaten garment validates questionable hanger appeal. Why hold on to a sweat-stained concert tee unless Joey Ramone actually spat on it? Surely that makes it a collector's item?

And therein lies the rub. The waves of nostalgia that flood her brain seem to have short-circuited the channels of logic. The fact that 99% of her closet's contents are too tatty to qualify for charity-shop status means she spends a lot of time in the other 1% looking wistfully on the memories of the past with little space for the future.

She kept a leopard print catsuit for ten years because an ex-boyfriend told her she looked fierce in it. Of course, what she really resembled was Pat Butcher on a kinky weekend and now that she's had a child, it looks even worse. Scary as it is, she can't even bring herself to wear it at Halloween, but she refuses to part with it. Its presence serves as a visual reminder of her youth (and lithe pre-pregnancy body).

Like a bad relationship, she holds on to clothes in the hopes that she can somehow make them work. That fringed poncho she wore at college still remains – despite having the festival kudos of a suburban housewife (she thought Burning Man was an STD).

As for the spandex trousers she was wearing when she first met her partner, she reckons she could still squeeze into them with a wire hanger and an inhaler. And her favourite threadbare cardigan? It comes in handy when doing gardening – even though she owns four perfectly intact alternatives. Deep down she knows she'd benefit from letting go, but the prospect of change is too daunting. One woman's trash, after all …

Black Widow

The most common closet type, and thus the most deadly, Black Widow casts a shroud over any attempt at individuation. What's more, she's got back-up. Armed with an arsenal of tried and trusted epithets – slimming, goes with everything, you're always dressed in … – not to mention hardcore practitioners like Coco Chanel, this lady's got the upper hand on why she can't (and won't) change.

Black Widow has a lot of black trousers. How many? Last count: 22. Don't judge. There's a perfectly legitimate explanation. For three years while in college, she worked part-time as a waitress, during which period she acquired a fail-safe wardrobe of black separates. After she graduated, her dark habit followed her: first job, first dates, parents' anniversary, best friend's wedding – basically every milestone imaginable apart from the obvious. Ah yes, the bitter irony.

Although funeral-ready, no one has actually died (unless you want to count her fashion mojo). Yes, her closet has all the hallmarks of the *Twilight* costume department. And yes, she needs a flashlight to get dressed. But that doesn't seem to deter her while shopping. Invariably, she veers towards the familiarity of black and its attendant safety. The idea of test-driving a bright colour or print scares her – not to mention the fact that she has absolutely no clue of how to style it.

In some cases, Black Widow's pattern is unintentional, a by-product of habit – but nonetheless one which is difficult to crack. As a result, she feels powerless to break the cycle that she's in. She's like the fashion undead – without the perks of a hot vampire boyfriend.

Split Personality

Split Personality has many guises: leather lover, conventional careerist, weekend countryphile, sporadic hipster – and a wardrobe for each. Non-committal and indecisive, her many moods dictate what she wears, resulting in ever-decreasing space and a compartmentalised, splintered dress sense.

In fact, Split Personality doesn't choose her clothes; they choose her. She's never been the type to pre-plan tomorrow's outfit, opt for hand luggage on a weekend flight or describe her look in less than three words. As for those who claim to take five minutes getting dressed in the morning, she simply doesn't trust them.

She does worry about her closet habits, though. Her one-bed apartment is a de facto walk-in wardrobe (only terribly disorganised) with little room for much else, let alone her seasonal trousseaux.

Truth be told, her mother had to convert the granny flat to store her tennis and skiing gear, not to mention all that paraphernalia from her clay pigeon shooting phase and last year's cobalt obsession, whcih could have rivalled that of Picasso on a good day, but enough said about that …

Split Personality simply can't choose just one trend, as the others hold equal possibilities. So she refrains from making the ultimate sacrifice by leaving all her options on the table. The drawback to this is that a real connection with a particular style never develops, leaving Split Personality in fashion limbo.

Martyr Mom

Martyr Mom hates shopping. Well, that's what she says. She'll pay top shekels to dress her clan but she remains threadbare to the bitter end. She'd be stealing food from her children's mouths, after all, and what kind of mother does that? Even though her youngest child is 19 (and quite capable of dressing himself), her legacy of self-denial and its associated badge of honour holds dominion over her closet. As she says herself, 'I'd give you the clothes off my back'. The question is: could you be bothered taking them?

Truth is, she loves getting done up but the martyr syndrome, passed down the gene pool by her own mother, has put the kibosh on anything more than hand-me-downs and 'this'll do'. The global recession was a bit of a boon, staving off the wicked spectre of self-interest. Excuses such as 'Do you think I'm made of money?' helped dig that rut a bit deeper, lest she had any notions of escaping.

The odd time when she does veer off the beaten path, guilt consumes her like a tsunami and the self-flagellation begins: 'I'm fine with what I have'; 'Sure who'd be looking at me anyway?'

Confusing selfishness with self-care, Martyr Mom doesn't have the confidence to invest in her own sartorial well-being – with the exception of regular underwear purchases (in case she gets run over by a bus). The result? A closet full of relics fit for a saint.

Sale Sniper

Sale Sniper is one highly trained marksman. Skilled in the art of retail warfare, she uses detailed field reconnaissance and stealth tactics to secure any and every available discount.

This lady understands that a successful target acquisition depends on several factors: an early start, sustained caffeine and blood sugar levels and knowing the shop assistants on a first-name basis. Not averse to using combat force (elbows do nicely) and counter-sniper tactics to get what she wants, no mission is ever impossible. First through the door of the January sales? Done. Gazumping at eBay auctions? Pah! Child's play.

Sadly, her single-minded focus means that quantity often trumps quality (they don't call it a haul for nothing) and thus a signature style is lacking.

Once her war stories have worn thin (three for the price of two! VIP discount! Free with every purchase, one to be moisturiser!), Sale Sniper invariably resigns her bargain rail booty to the charity pile. The thrill of the till means her real needs miss the mark, leaving her closet to bear the battle scars.

Perfect 9

Perfect 9 is a rare breed – the 2.3 kids and a white picket fence of closet happiness. Self-aware and perma-prepared, she's got an enviable handle on her shopping habits. Impulse buys and repeat purchases are what others do – not this lady. Her wardrobe is so damn organised, it makes the IKEA catalogue look like amateur hour. Control – that's how she rolls.

Ironically, it's this impeccable precision that stops Perfect 9 from being a perfect 10. The pursuit of perfection is often sought at the expense of personality and while pleased with her balanced capsule of basics and trends, she's prone to becoming a tad complacent and, dare we say, predictable.

Before you know it, Perfect 9 is stuck in a rut of her own making and in a panic-bid to find her fun side, gives that batwing mini-dress the glad eye and sneaks off to the changing room for a quickie. Sure, there's no harm in trying it on, now is there? Unless of course she buys it ... and hides it ... and feels guilt-ridden every time she looks at it. The shame, oh the shame. If taking things for granted is her Achilles heel, then learning to keep the love alive is her arch support.

THE CLOSET QUIZ

'Know thyself and dress accordingly.'

EPICTETUS

Have you identified yourself clearly in the line-up? Perhaps you relate to more than one type? Don't panic. This is all perfectly normal. As the evolutionary propensity to hoard underpins much of our closet turmoil, there will invariably be shared characteristics. Think of it as a fashion horoscope. Although your dominant traits may belong to one closet type, an ascendant and moon sign also play a supporting role.

Still unsure? Take the Closet Quiz to clarify:
- Your core closet type
- Your position on the Happy Closet Spectrum
- Your dominant shopping patterns
- The excuses enabling your habit.

Q1 YOU'RE GOING SHOPPING TODAY. WHAT DO YOU DO BEFORE YOU HIT THE SHOPS?

a) Make a list of the items I need so that I don't waste money on panic buys or unplanned purchases.

b) Gather my credit cards and pray that there's a bit of wiggle room left after my Net-a-Porter splurge last week. Note to self: never mix wine and Wi-Fi!

c) Remove the mirror over the fireplace and check there's room left in the secret safe for a new stash. How my husband hasn't cottoned on to this is anyone's guess!

d) Call up the carpenter. Time to convert the guest room into a walk-in wardrobe.

e) Make a cup of tea, call my mother, do some laundry and put off the inevitable. I hate shopping. It's too stressful. Besides, what I have is grand. It'll do.

f) Comb through the fashion magazines and decide which trends I'm going to follow this season. Granted, red doesn't suit my complexion and I don't have the legs for '60s-style minis – but fashion is fashion.

g) What do you mean? When in doubt, buy a black dress!

h) See what the kids need, even though they're grown up and married with their own kids.

i) Create a strategic sales map and engage target at 0900 hours.

YOU'RE ON THE HIGH STREET WITH A CREDIT CARD AND A CLEAR SCHEDULE (NO KIDS, NO HUSBAND, NO WORRIES). WHAT HAPPENS NEXT?

a) I follow my list, ticking things off with military precision. I won't buy something for the sake of it. If it's not the right fit, it can wait. What's important is to buy only those things that I know I'll wear and love.

b) Something resembling *Supermarket Sweep*. I've generally blown the budget within the first hour on things I love but don't need. Speaking of which, I still haven't got round to getting new knickers.

c) I see those Sophia Webster shoes and take a look at the price tag. €850. Gulp. I can't drop a digit on these when divulging the price to my husband – too risky. I do a quick dimensions scan. I can easily stash these away in the back of the wardrobe without him noticing for a few months – then, when I pull them out, I can legitimately say I've had them for ages. Everyone wins.

d) Oh, I like that sweater; I'll take one in every colour. Oh, I like that dress; I'll take one in every print. Oh, I like those shoes; I'll take a pair in every colour. Oh, there's no room in the car …

e) In the unlikely event that I do get dragged out shopping, I'll find a nice charity shop in which to pass the time. The smell of moth balls is comforting.

f) Carnage.

g) The usual. I vow to try something different and get totally bamboozled by choice – so I find the nearest black dress, pay for it and go home.

h) I go window-shopping. The pane of glass helps separate me from my guilt. Besides, what reason do I have to get all decked out?

i) I go straight to the sale rails. The only thing that turns me on is when I get money off.

Q3 YOU RETURN FROM YOUR SHOPPING TRIP. TIME TO EMPTY YOUR BAGS AND EXAMINE YOUR PURCHASES. WHICH WORD GROUP IS MOST LIKELY TO GO THROUGH YOUR HEAD?

a) Pleased–satisfied–confident

b) Unique–noticed–individual

c) Hide–stash–hoard

d) Stockpile–amass–collect

e) Comfort–safety–familiar

f) Channelling–inspired–alter ego

g) Same–old–thing

h) Martyr–saint–sacrifice

i) Bargain–discount–deal

HOW OFTEN DO YOU FEEL REMORSEFUL AFTER HAVING BOUGHT SOMETHING?

a) When I fall prey to the odd impulse buy, which is infrequent, thankfully.

b) When the buzz wears off or if I don't get enough compliments wearing it.

c) When I allow myself to think about it, which I don't.

d) When someone asks me how much I paid for it.

e) What's remorse?

HOW MANY OF THE EXCUSES BELOW HAVE YOU USED WHEN JUSTIFYING A PURCHASE YOU DON'T NEED/CAN'T AFFORD?

a) I don't make excuses. I never buy anything that I don't need or use.

b) It was too pretty to pass up.

c) Don't need to. No one ever finds out.

d) You can never have too many (insert random item here).

e) It reminds me of that time when …

f) I need it for my aerial yoga class/Tibetan sound bowl workshop/dinner party this weekend (delete as appropriate).

g) You're always dressed in black.

h) Never. The only excuses I make are for why I don't shop.

i) 5% off? Sure they were practically giving it away!

Q6 HOW MANY WARDROBES DO YOU USE?

a) One

b) Two

c) Three – not counting the attic, the closet under the stairwell, the kids' playroom and the laundry room

d) I've stopped counting

Q7 HOW MANY TIMES A YEAR DO YOU CLEAR OUT YOUR CLOSET?

a) Once

b) Once every six months

c) On a continual basis – about once a season

d) When there is absolutely no space left and I cannot shut the doors

e) Er … I can't remember

Q8 IF YOUR HOUSE WAS ROBBED OF ALL ITS CONTENTS, WHICH WOULD MAKE YOU MOST UPSET?

a) Losing your flat screen, laptop, credit cards, sound system and smartphone

b) Losing your entire wardrobe

IF YOU HAD TO GIVE UP SHOPPING TOMORROW, WHAT WOULD YOU REPLACE IT WITH?

a) A self-improvement class like yoga or Italian lessons that would widen my experiences

b) Crying

 WHICH IS MORE IMPORTANT?

a) Quality

b) Quantity

 WHICH GROUP OF WORDS IN THE LIST BELOW BEST DESCRIBES THE CURRENT STATE OF YOUR WARDROBE?

a) Organised, planned, unified

b) Chaotic, spontaneous, unco-ordinated

c) Secretive, hidden, guilty pleasure

d) Excessive, overstocked, emergency

e) Nostalgic, disjointed, worn out

f) Familiar, uniform, clinical

g) Eclectic, moody, random

h) Selfless, threadbare, austerity

i) Discount, disposable, detached

Q12 FINALLY, WRITE YOUR ANSWERS TO THE FOLLOWING QUESTIONS IN A JOURNAL (KEEP IT HANDY, YOU'LL BE USING IT AGAIN!):

a) What was your most regrettable purchase?

b) What purchase makes you happiest?

c) Which item in your closet gives you the best cost-per-wear value?

d) What item do you refuse to part with?

ANSWERS

QUESTIONS 1–3: YOUR CLOSET TYPE

- Your answers to Questions 1–3 reveals your closet type from the nine closet types: Impulse Buyer, Secret Shopper, Doomsday Prepper, Black Widow, Tired & Emotional, Split Personality, Martyr Mom, Sale Sniper and Perfect 9.

- Your answers to Questions 1 and 2 examine your attitude to shopping and your habits in the field.

- Your answer to Question 3 reveals your attitude (hidden or otherwise) to shopping.

Check your answers to Questions 1–3 against the types below. Remember: it's common to tick different letters for different questions. Some people possess qualities belonging to several types, while others are straight-up blue bloods. If you ticked:

a) Feel free to smile – you've put your closet in a good mood.

b) Impulse Buyer

c) Secret Shopper

d) Doomsday Prepper

e) Tired & Emotional

f) Split Personality

g) Black Widow

h) Martyr Mom

i) Sale Sniper

QUESTION 4: YOUR SELF-AWARENESS

Your answer to Question 4 examines the most important gauge of closet happiness: your feelings when the thrill of the till has worn off.

a) Well done. You exhibit some stellar control over your shopping habits with the odd misstep that you take measures to correct.

b) You allow others to validate your sense of self. Moreover, you achieve this through externals that, over time, become a self-perpetuating cycle. Trust me. Those Joneses are worse than the Kardashians.

c) I'd say you're in denial but you probably wouldn't believe me.

d) Your shopping habit has become so unconscious that it takes an external agent to bring you back to reality.

e) Oh dear. Your total lack of self-awareness means you probably skipped this question.

QUESTIONS 5–10: YOUR POSITION ON THE HAPPY CLOSET SPECTRUM

Your answer to Questions 5–10 determine your present position on the Happy Closet Spectrum from 1 to 10, 1 being Happiest, 10 being Unhappiest. Add up the points you get for each question to find your position on the Happy Closet Spectrum.

Question 5: Count the number of excuses you ticked and give yourself the following points:

- More than three excuses = 2 points
- Fewer than three excuses = 1 point
- Did you answer a)? Busted. Trick question! The more self-satisfied we are with our habits, the more likely we'll be tripped up by our unconscious mind. Need proof? Compare your answer to Question 5 with your answer to Question 11 – the current state of your wardrobe. You may not make excuses, but are you happy with the results? Unless you answered a) to Question 11, then some conscious awareness training is in order.

QUESTION 6:

a) 0

b) 1

c) 2

d) 2

QUESTION 7:

a) 1

b) 0

c) 0

d) 2

e) 3

QUESTION 8:

a) 0

b) 1

QUESTION 9:

a) 0

b) 1

QUESTION 10:

a) 0

b) 1

Now add up your points and find out where you sit on the Happy Closet Spectrum. The average score is 5. Scores below 5 warrant a high five, toast, Twitter hashtag and air of supreme smugness. Scores above 5 require some behavioural modification, which we'll address later.

QUESTION 11: YOUR CLOSET MANTRA

Your answer to Question 11 will generate your new closet mantra. The three words are the opposite of your current state – an achievable long-term goal. Recite them daily as an affirmation; programme them into your phone; post them inside the doors of your wardrobe, on the biscuit tin, on the wine rack – whatever you need to do to make your new mantra memorable.

a) You've already got your mantra sorted!

b) Harmonious, planned, co-ordinated

c) Open, visible, self-satisfied

d) Essential, self-assured, calm

e) Present tense, put-together, relevant

f) Diverse, colourful, textured

g) Cohesive, committed, decisive

h) Self-care, fresh, indulgent

i) Premium, cherished, necessary

QUESTION 12:

Your answers to the different parts of Question 12 provide an insight into your shopping weaknesses and strengths:

❖ Your most regrettable purchase relates to a sense of loss on account of a questionable past decision. Most common answers include (but are not limited to): items that cost a fortune but have never been worn; clothes that don't fit well; and anything bought in haste for an event or to please someone else (insert friend's wedding here).

❖ Your happiest purchase is the flipside to the purchase you find most regrettable. Common answers include (but are not limited to): well-priced items worn regularly; items that evokes a feeling of comfort or bliss (fleece PJs or flocked satin ballgown – take your pick); and anything that hustles in a good compliment or three.

❖ Your cost-per-wear ratio shines a light on that which you value most – the staples that keep you looking 'put-together'. Common answers include (but are not limited to): jeans; casual shoes and boots; tops and sweaters; and winter coats. That's not to say your latex kinky boots don't give you good value if you wear them religiously. Everyone is different, and 'amen' to that!

❖ Finally, those things you refuse to part with generally fall into two categories: keepsakes or keeping something for the sake of it. Common answers include (but are not limited to): wedding dresses; pieces inherited from parents or grandparents; vintage items; random nostalgic memorabilia; and 'I'll diet back into that if it kills me' clothing.

Bookmark this page, my lovelies, because we'll be elaborating on your Question 12 answers throughout each chapter. Why are they so important? Well, even the happiest closets reveal moments of weakness. Just because you make lists, follow them and are pleased with your purchases, you may not necessarily be giving your closet what it needs. You may have answered mostly a) to Questions 1–3 and your mantra may be already be 'organised, planned, unified', but that regrettable purchase is more than just an innocuous flub – it blows the lid on the unconscious leanings that create wardrobe woes.

Surprised? Indignant? Need a cuddle? Yes, the process is a bit of a shocker, but if self-awareness were that easy, we'd all be as mindful as a temple of Buddhist monks. The truth is we are the sum total of the choices we make – good and bad. Nonetheless, the brain doesn't like to think it makes bad decisions. After all, we've got bragging rights on everything from careers to travel escapades to high-flying finance. Why is it, then, that we can't seem to get a grip on our closet happiness? The answer? Three simple words: too much choice. That's what has you in this spot of bother. The easiest way to manage choice (and its kissing cousin, regret) is in knowing who you are. So get ready to dig deep because now that we've unlocked those closet doors, the real change can begin.

Let's face it. We've all got our demons and unless you're operating some kind of *Poltergeist* portal to the dead, this process should be more purgative than purgatorial. The real trick in creating long-term closet calm isn't about willpower (we'll get to that in the next chapter); it's about understanding the emotional pay-off that has you haunted year after year through the same closet hang-ups. Isolate your triggers and you've got a decent shot at peace and harmony.

CHAPTER TWO

OLD HABITS DIE HARD

HOW TO CHANGE THE HABITS OF A LIFETIME

'The fixity of a habit is generally in direct proportion to its absurdity.'

MARCEL PROUST

was 26 and working as a recruitment consultant during Ireland's Celtic Tiger years when life was a party and work was, well, not a lot like work. I had graduated from university, dabbled in some teaching and, on the advice of a friend, decided it was time for me to get suited and booted and join the corporate world. Recruitment, I was told, would hustle a nice chunk of change and set me up to be a woman of independent means. I could be a business dynamo by day and writer by candlelit night – ah, the glamour of it all. Not quite.

I couldn't place a candidate if my livelihood depended on it – and, funnily enough, it did. For the record, the one 'score' I did make failed to turn up on her first day at work. She 'didn't feel like it' apparently. The numbers clearly weren't stacked in my favour. I was in the wrong job and in no position to be aiding the careers of others. How they let me continue for nine months without firing my sorry ass is anyone's guess. Suffice to say, I spent the guts of a year avoiding eye contact with my supervisor and holding out for a small but welcome monthly pay cheque.

Despite the fact that I was a P45 waiting to happen, I blew away much of my (in)disposable income on a fleeting retail high: vertiginous snakeskin boots, Studio 54 jumpsuits, burlesque bustiers and ridiculous fripperies. The more removed from my mundane existence the better. The bag of cheap swag, however (my finances were more Primark than Prada), wasn't really the end-game. It was the emotional pay-off that had me hooked.

I was celebrating avoiding the sack, while at the same time compensating for the fact that I was a failure in my ill-chosen field. Each monthly bank transfer triggered the same scenario: the building anticipation, a heady shopping fling, followed by a brief climax and the walk of shame. And so it continued ...

My habit became so ingrained that I chose to ignore the evidence that I wasn't, in fact, a trustafarian, heir to the Getty dynasty or a woman of any means – let alone of the independent variety. Instead, I had a corporate job, a circus performer's closet and a current account that permanently read 'insufficient funds'.

When I did decide to resign (much to the relief of my employer) and find a more fulfilling role in publishing, my habit didn't quit. Nah, it was only warming up. I had those neuropathways well and truly trod. In fact, shopping had become more of an automatic response than an anticipated reward.

Upon moving to London a few years later, my Oxford Street office was a gift-wrapped excuse for indulging in regular retail therapy. As soon as I walked into a department store (hello Selfridges!), those pesky basal ganglia would kick in, identifying the habit I'd stored in my brain related to shopping. It wasn't that I needed anything or, in fact, wanted anything. The spendthrift autopilot in my head, however, had other plans and invariably I'd emerge, bag in hand, wondering what the hell just happened.

And so it continued: bags were filled, wallets were emptied and I was still none the happier – that is until I got my reality check (which thankfully didn't bounce) and turned my closet around. You're probably nodding your head in empathy. Well, we can nod together like bobble-head dogs on a car dashboard or we can get stuck into some handy hacks for reprogramming those wayward shopping habits. I'm taking it that you're nodding in agreement. OK. Let's do this.

TRIGGERS AND WILLPOWER

'Willpower is trying very hard not to do something you
very much want to do.'

JOHN ORTBERG

Willpower is misunderstood. The very word suggests that
wanting something badly enough bequeaths the necessary
strength to achieve or overcome something. If that were the
case, I'd be Michael Fassbender's missus by now. The other
misconception about willpower is that once mitigated by
temptation, it is irretrievably lost to some esoteric ether.

Here's the thing: willpower is more of a muscle than a virtue.
What's more, it's self-regulating and will atrophy if left to sit in
the bargain basement of your brain. Willpower is self-control
and self-control isn't sexy. Wild abandon, on the other hand, is
pretty hot. Nothing turns us on more than wanting something
we can't (or shouldn't) have. Think of it. Would you continue
to leaf through a Mills & Boon novel that read: 'Miranda started
to arch her back like an alley cat but thought better of it and
buttoned up her dress instead. Fabio always did admire her
Calvinist restraint.' Not exactly a bodice-ripper, is it?

In order to create real change, not the flimsy kind that is
rationalised away by the prospect of a sale or pseudo-need, it's

necessary to replace negative patterns with new positive ones – a process referred to as 'reframing'.

Given that it takes a little over two months for a habit to stick (just ask habit guru James Clear), you can bet that weakness for La Perla knickers is already firmly encoded in the old grey matter. Such is 'the force of habit' (and its colloquial sway) that the brain clings to it at the expense of common sense, which would explain the ineffable appeal of harem pants, snow-wash denim and hipster glasses.

As the old saying goes, 'It's with the best intentions that the worst work is done'. In other words, the stronger the habit, the more likely it is to overrule our conscious intention, however well-intended.

Avoiding department stores, boutiques and the high street when you have a full wallet and an empty stomach simply isn't enough. Internet shopping, smartphones and tablets have created an immediacy that feeds into our hang-ups and leads to regular bouts of retail amnesia. I like to call it 'trigger happy' – but as we all know, triggers rarely leave us happy; in fact, they tend, more often than not, to leave a gaping hole in our wallets and wardrobes. You know the story: add to cart, subtract from wallet, multiply to wardrobe, divide into charity bags.

What can be done with the help of some mindfulness techniques is to overpower the offending practice by reshaping it – habit bootcamp, if you will. Charles Duhigg, author of *The Power of Habit*, recommends controlling our habits by changing the cues that set them off. Once the cues, or triggers, have been identified, it's a question of delivering a 'competing response' – something with personal resonance that will distract you when your willpower muscle is clapped out (after resisting Fabio's advances).

The power to change starts with First Response Training, an honest assessment of your actions and reactions while out shopping. Tapping into these emotional reflexes will help you isolate the triggers that hijack your hormones and leave you in a state of sartorial emergency. So keep your pen and paper handy and prepare for the truth, the whole truth and nothing but the truth. (Uncross those fingers – I see you!)

FIRST RESPONSE TRAINING

'If you tell the truth, you don't have to remember anything.'

MARK TWAIN

First Response Training helps aid and assist our feelings while out in the field. As most of us are either unconscious or emotional shoppers, it's easier to get clarity on how we behave when removed from the situation. The following visualisation exercise, which starts by imagining a typical shopping scenario, helps identify your personal pitfalls and craft a competing response. Consider it conscious awareness training in action.

Let's get started. Close your eyes and imagine yourself shopping. Build a mental picture of how it looks, sounds, smells and feels; hold the image in your head, and then answer the following questions:

- What is your emotional state when you go shopping? Are you tired? Over-excited? Stressed? Overwhelmed?
- When do you usually shop? At weekends? After work? Late-night shopping? On the fly?
- Who do you normally shop with? Are you alone? With a family member? With the entire family?
- Use your five senses to fill in your shopping scenario. Is it filled with screaming children? Are the queues for the changing rooms long or short? Is there music playing? Can you get parking?
- Now think about the feelings that accompany this picture. Are you relaxed or in a hurry? Do you take in everything around you? Stash and grab, make discerning purchases or get befuddled and leave?
- When you get home do you feel a sense of accomplishment or despair? Have you ticked off most or all of what's on your list? Do you even have a list?

In the table on the next page, list each of these sensations under the heading TRIGGERS: for example, tired, stressed, tempted.

In the next column, illustrate your typical response to each:

- When I'm tired – I buy what I don't need.
- When I'm stressed – I buy too much.
- When I'm tempted – I'll convince myself I need it even if I don't.
- When I am unsure – I get flustered and come home empty-handed.

In the last column, put the new habit that will reframe your shopping experience:

- When I am tempted, I usually go sale shopping and buy a bunch of things I don't need simply because they have been discounted.
- The next time I feel tempted by a sale, I am going to grab a coffee and think about whether I really do need it, how many things it goes with, whether I can I afford it and whether, by next month, I will still really love it.

TRIGGER	TYPICAL RESPONSE	NEW HABIT

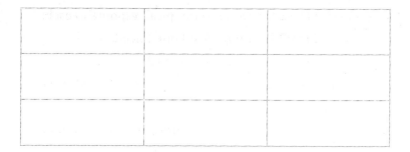

You've now identified your first response to shopping situations and come up with a competing response to help you break your shopping habits. Self-help support groups call this 'interrupting the acting out' or envisioning the *future* result behind the *present* temptation:

> If I buy these €200 suede sandals, I'll probably wear them to a wedding this summer and then they will sit in the back of my wardrobe for the rest of the year. The last time I bought a similar pair, the baby threw up on them and the dog used them as a chew toy … and then threw up.

Next, think even more about your responses above and ask yourself:

- If shopping makes you feel more confident/more calm/ more in control, how do you feel when you don't get an opportunity to shop/don't find what you want in your size/don't find that sweater featured in this month's *Vogue*?

- If bidding on eBay makes you feel accomplished/
  excited, how do you feel when you are outbid/when you
  don't get a chance to go online?

Often when we don't get what we want, when the anticipated high doesn't follow the trigger, we fall foul to a hollow hankering, persistent thoughts and borderline obsessive behaviour. Sound familiar? Of course it does. Cravings are the cornerstone of every habit – good and bad. Without them, athletes wouldn't strive to beat a personal best, lovers wouldn't cross oceans and seas to be together and shoppers wouldn't give sales assistants their mobile number on the off-chance that those limited edition Stella McCartney flatforms happen to be reordered in a size 8 (ahem, insert red face here). So what can a gal do when she gets that familiar urge?

CONSTANT CRAVING

'Gretchen, stop trying to make "fetch" happen! It's not
going to happen!'

REGINA GEORGE, *MEAN GIRLS*

My sister has a borderline unhealthy obsession with skinny white jeans. To clarify, she doesn't actually own a pair but lives in hope that she'll find one that says 'boarding a private jet to Necker Island' as opposed to 'Hollywood Boulevard street-walker'. The fact is: this figment exists strictly in her imagination. She's tried upwards of 100 pairs, has seen the evidence and still insists that obliterating her self-esteem is somehow preferable to cutting her losses. Such is their loaded significance (Hamptons living, breezy Michael Kors campaigns), she is willing to put reality on hold in order to fulfil this future projection of sartorial bliss. All this does is cause her pain – be it carpal tunnel or tunnelling to Bloomingdales in the New York mid-winter snow (yes, this actually happened). White jeans, like Gretchen Weiners's 'fetch', just aren't going to happen. My sister knows this, yet she hinges her closet happiness on the pursuit of this self-styled Holy Grail, wasting time and energy craving the very thing she can't have.

Our feelings, as visceral as they can be, are ultimately short-lived. The consequences of acting on said feelings, sadly, are not. Identifying the craving driving your actions is key to pumping the brakes and letting logic take the wheel. By cataloguing your past mistakes, missteps and misadventures, and using First Response Training to come up with a way to avoid them in the future, you'll be in a better position to understand the present chronology of what Charles Duhigg describes as the cue–habit–reward loop and cut the emotional trip-wire before falling foul of another wardrobe woe.

If you don't already keep a journal or diary, there's no time like the present. Consider it your personal *Burn Book*

– a place to vent sartorial spleen, to unleash on gormless garments and get clear on your fashion feelings. Keeping note of how each shopping event actually plays out in all of its inglorious Technicolor will create a memorable tether to every unsuccessful purchase. Make it gory. I mean really dish the dirt. Don't be afraid of a bit of spew. The more you regurgitate the nasty parts to yourself, the quicker they will become embedded in the noggin as a red flag. Here it goes. Prepare to put that itchy finger to good use …

TYPICAL TRIGGERS

- Make a list of past garments that have caused you pain. Grab boxes of old photos, check your social media pages and ferret out anything that may be lurking in the darker recesses of your wardrobe or house (the attic, the boiler, beneath the floorboards).

- Index each item according to its discomfort type, e.g. physical: those jeans that can only be worn with the help of cocoa butter and a decade of the rosary; emotional: that bedazzled coin-hemmed kimono that makes you look like a rodeo clown; financial: the dress you bought for €500 to wear to your ex-boyfriend's wedding and never wore again – who's the clown now?

- Next to each item, create a column listing the visual, emotional and external triggers (the person or event) that motivated the action and another column listing the final outcome of your purchase.

Feeling shy? Allow me to take the lead.

ITEM	PAIN TYPE	VISUAL TRIGGER	EMOTIONAL TRIGGER	EXTERNAL TRIGGER	FINAL SCENARIO
Jeans	Physical	That long-limbed Scandinavian model in the ad campaign.	Longing – I needed jeans that gave me those legs!	The sales assistant telling me to buy the last pair (even though they weren't in my size) as they had 'good stretch'.	Still unworn in the wardrobe; still a size too small; still no sign of the mythical 'good stretch'.
Jacket	Emotional	The sparkles – oh the sparkles – gimme gimme gimme some sparkles!	Excitement – I needed something to cheer me up.	My sister telling me to buy it while at the till paying for her own guilty stash.	Still unworn in the wardrobe; still feeling too silly to return it.
Dress	Financial	The killer price tag #marriedtochanel	Revenge – I needed a dress that said 'I'm over you!'	My ex-boyfriend's wedding.	Still haven't worn it since his wedding five years ago when my wearable mortgage repayment went entirely unnoticed.

Now it's your turn. Open your journal and write out your own personal experiences, taking care to include each sequential trigger. Context is vital to habitual behaviour as we tend to perform the same actions in response to certain situations. Then examine the collective proof. Take a highlighter and underline the verbs and adjectives that define the tone of the story. Do this with every item on your list. What do you see? Can you see a thread emerging? Certain patterns? These are the triggers that need to be addressed in order to create happier shopping habits.

> I bought that coin-hemmed parrot print kimono because **I felt fat** and wanted something **distracting** (achieved) to cover my bum. It caught my eye straight away. When **I asked my sister** how I looked, she told me I looked 'amazing' (with her back turned while at the till, paying for her own guilty stash). **I was afraid** if I didn't buy it then, they wouldn't have my size (one shop assistant said it was limited edition; another said it was 'running out the door'). I was really keen on something **to cheer me up**, so I bought it. When I got home, I realised I looked like I was auditioning for a part in *Priscilla, Queen of the Desert* and I was just too deflated to bother returning it.

Now that you've used the past to understand your closet hang-ups and habits, it's up to you to create future closet happiness by coming up with a competing response. Let's develop the

First Response Training exercise even further and get a more detailed working manifesto in place:

- Whenever I feel fat, I'm going to do something constructive like go for a mood-enhancing walk or yoga session rather than go shopping. When I do go shopping, I'll make sure to check in with my feelings before I make a purchase. I've made too many bad choices by buying things to improve my mood.

- I'm going to try shopping alone rather than bringing others with me. People tend to have their own agenda (and are usually concentrating on what they want) so I'm told what I want to rather than need to hear. If I really need a second opinion, I'll bring Joanne. Her absolute lack of a filter and pitying poker face could prove pretty useful.

You see? That didn't hurt, now did it? What *will* hurt is if your short-term memory short-circuits the next time you find yourself locked in a dressing room, panting and half-naked, with an arm full of clothes. All it takes is for one seemingly innocent excuse ('Just trying it on!') to run ramshackle over your resolutions. Before you know it, you'll be stashing that new black dress (to add to the other ten you already own) in your dismounted soap box, convincing yourself it was a small indiscretion. *But was it?*

HAPPINESS HACK

What's the worst crime you've committed in order to get what you wanted? In other words, what sneaky misdemeanours are you guilty of on account of your craving? Bribed a shop assistant? Body-checked an old lady to get to that last pair of shoes in your size? Need someone to share first? Let's get some next-level shame on the boards to help oil those honesty cogs. I know there's a story in there somewhere ...

CONTENT WARNING: *The following account contains scenes that may have been created for your entertainment.*

♥ Shovelling snow out of the driveway at 4 a.m. to arrive early at the January sales.
♥ Queuing in the snow at the January sales (with shovel).
♥ Using said shovel to create a clear path while running through the aisles to grab that Balenciaga bag.
♥ Being apprehended by security for brandishing a potential weapon in a public space.
♥ Being mug-shot in the local police station and cautioned for disorderly conduct.
♥ Being instructed not to come within a 100-foot radius of said retail establishment.
♥ Having my mother find out on the local news.
♥ Being branded the official family black sheep.
♥ Unable to look at Italian leather without flashbacks.
  Let it out, honey. Put it in the Burn Book ...

EXCUSES, EXCUSES, EXCUSES

'Two wrongs don't make a right, but they make a good excuse.'

THOMAS STEPHEN SZASZ

Excuses – the great enabler. Without them, we'd have no reason to shop when we shouldn't and every reason to feel guilty for doing so. Nothing like the aul' 'dog ate my knickers' chestnut to manifest a new handbag at will (in which to deposit much-needed new knickers, of course).

If triggers are to willpower what a finger is to a loaded gun, then excuses are the bullets that blow a hole in our accountability. Rock, paper, scissors, folks. Truth be told, being the victim isn't so bad. When you've got a metaphorical Smith & Wesson aimed at your head, choice suddenly becomes an obligation: you *had* to buy those leather trousers; you *couldn't* leave the shop without a princess headband; and you'd simply *die* if you didn't get a pair of those over-the-knee boots.

Don't try and fool me, kiddo – I'm on to you! You see, I was once in your overpriced shoes, only more armed and dangerous than most. Having moved home, away from the lure of London's high streets, I continued to fan the flames of my habit by taking up work as a stylist. (Clever, that!) I hid behind a wall of work-appropriate excuses that granted me a degree of immunity (or so I thought) in the course of my official duties. Call it an occupational hazard, or call it self-deception. Either way, my handy one-liners ('I bought it for a photoshoot'; 'I can't help it, I work in fashion!') prevented me from connecting in a meaningful way with my own reality (rather than that of Anna Wintour).

I worked from my kitchen table in a two-up two-down terraced house close to Dublin's inner city. I took the bus to meetings and carried a trolley-dolly around town to pull clothes. I ate lunch in local cafés boasting free Wi-Fi and took great pleasure in redeeming a free coffee on my loyalty card at the end of most weeks (and still do). Not exactly Manhattan's Upper East Side, lunching in Balthazar and being chauffeur-driven to talk shop with Marc Jacobs. Mine was a more humble reality, which I seemed behoven to elevate through my ever-expanding wardrobe.

There was obviously a gap between my real and imagined self and this emotional conflict played out in rational lies – the logic I superimposed on my feelings of inadequacy. There's a big difference between dressing yourself and dressing the person you think you should be. One is a person; the other is a hologram. My actions didn't reflect my true motivations. I was still suffering from the same impostor syndrome as I did hustling human resources. It was up to me to clean that up. Buying all this stuff was simply covering the guilt track. Self-serving in logic, self-destructive at heart.

Seemingly innocent but actually insidious, excuses, over time, prevent us from true closet accountability. Can you think of a good reason for everything you've bought? Can you remember a time when you caught yourself out in an excuse? Yes? Good! This simple act of awareness is the first step in removing the roadblocks and getting your closet in gear. It's up to you to put your foot on the accelerator.

Do these sound familiar?

I need to buy ~~tights and underwear~~ shoes that I can't walk in without a tightrope bar.

I have nothing to wear at weekends.

I have nothing to wear to work.

I have nothing to wear out.

New? I've had these for ~~ages~~ two days.

These are my 'Don't you want to rent me this apartment?' pants (see: *Friends* Season 6, Episode 3).

This jacket is ideal for walking the dog (note: does not have dog).

I need it for my job.

I need it for my sanity.

I need it to get a new job.

I just need it, OK!

My dog ate the contents of my wardrobe (note: still does not have dog).

I need to break in this new credit card.

I'm just looking … really.

I'm holding it for a friend.

50% off? That means you can buy two!

I feel fat.

I'm helping the economy.

It's cheaper than therapy.

I'm actually a mystery shopper. Don't blow my cover.

It's an investment buy.

I don't shop often but when I do, I like to buy ~~quality~~ expensive sh*t
I don't need.

It's late-night shopping.

I'm drunk.

I've been framed.

I'm doing research into the dark underbelly of shopping addiction.

I mistakenly pressed the 'buy now' button and before I knew it, the
item had been dispatched. Hey ho, waddayagonnado?

My aura specialist tells me red is bad for my energy field. I've got to
stock up on some blues and greens … fast!

Define 'need' …

HAPPINESS HACK

Can't tell an excuse from a reason? Sounds like an excuse to me.
The next time you find yourself planning a pity party on account
of being busted with shopping bags, consider this:

A reason is an explanation.
An excuse is a justification.

A reason takes responsibility.
An excuse blames.

A reason tells the truth.
An excuse tells a rational lie.

A reason serves a purpose.
An excuse serves itself.

WHAT'S THE PAY-OFF?

'Whether we like it or not, we are puppets of our emotions. We make complex decisions by consulting our feelings, not our thoughts. Against our best intentions, we substitute the question, "What do I think about this?" with "How do I feel about this?"'

ROLF DOBELLI, *THE ART OF THINKING CLEARLY*

I remember running into Zara one evening after a particularly awful networking event. I was trying to fend off the flashbacks of having made a total fool of myself 20 minutes earlier and buying a soft sweater in which to smother my mortification seemed a good bet – if not an ironic one. Let me fill you in.

I arrived at this champagne-and-diamonds affair, hosted by a colleague and attended by a room full of strangers. It was a November evening and unseasonably warm. Despite the mercury rising, I was clad in cashmere and felted wool. Having arrived in a bit of a rush, I was already slightly flushed and a tad apprehensive about knowing nobody in the room.

The fact that the majority of people at this party were stockbrokers and financial advisers did little to assuage my insecurity. I was labouring over what I would say when I arrived, not knowing the Dow Index from my own index finger. And in short, the one person I spoke to walked away from me while I was introducing myself.

Not that I blame the woman. I was sweating like Christy Moore at a Feis Ceoil, so badly, in fact, that I looked like I was sporting a finger moustache as I attempted to rescue suicidal perspiration drops from my upper lip. Classy.

Then suddenly I felt a tap on my shoulder. I turned to face a rather pleasant woman who looked like she might actually be interested in staying long enough to catch my name. 'Hello,' I grinned through my pretend facial hair. 'So sorry,' she apologised, 'I thought I'd just let you know you've got lipstick on your teeth'. And with that, walked away. Although impressed that she managed to spot the smear of Russian Red through my crafty disguise, I felt my poor ego deflate like a whoopee cushion – only this was far less funny. I was the tall sweaty girl with lipstick on her teeth standing alone in the middle of a crowded room and showing some curious love for Movember. There was no recovery. It was time to leave.

Before I had time to even process the mild emotional whiplash, I found myself escaping into the late-night shopping arms of my inconstant yet delicious lover. My pay-off was a self-esteem boost; my pay-out was a 9.5% APR on my MasterCard. Was it worth it? Hardly. Filling my closet was really a stand-in for how I felt about myself. Shopping provided me with the elusive feel-good factor that I longed for. It wasn't about the clothes I was wearing; it was about what they represented. Individually, they symbolised respect, admiration, acceptance; collectively, they epitomised my own internal jumble sale.

Facing the full-length mirror of self-awareness wasn't about holding a truth stick and talking about my feelings. I was only able to tackle my seemingly unshakeable shopping habits when I got to grips with the fact that clothes really weren't the reward. It was up to me to confront my emotional pay-off or continue paying the price.

Habit-meister and founder of PsyBlog (psyblog.co.uk) Jeremy Dean sums this up nicely in his best-selling tome *Making Habits, Breaking Habits: How to Make Changes that Stick*, 'As we repeat our behaviours, what we're learning is an association between our actions and their outcomes.'

Cause and effect, folks: as creatures of habit, our unconscious drives us towards the stimulus that gives us the desired response – regardless of the knock-on effect or how it aligns with our long-term goals. In fact, what I've spent on clothing (much of which has made its way into charity bags and recycling bins over the years) could have made a decent dent in a down-payment on a new house or a six-month career break to trek around South East Asia and the Pacific Islands.

The lifespan of material fulfilment is short at best. It peaks sharply and then evens out once we've adjusted to its presence. Think of all the times you 'had to have' something, only to forget you even had it a few months later. Ironically, when we indulge in our shopping habit with greater regularity and, as a result, our Pavlovian response becomes more automatic (new sweater = retail high), the theraputic act of the purchase becomes distanced from the retail act with the experience ultimately losing its cachet. The first step to change? Being aware of the infinite power the unconscious holds in guiding our thinking and changing our behaviour.

It's not all doom and gloom. The beauty about a craving is that it can be marshalled to serve our greater good. Cravings make it easier to push through difficulties. If we focus on the feeling associated with the reward (self-esteem, accomplishment) and apply it to something more meaningful, we can manage back the offending habit.

So here's your chance to go deep – really deep. Open up that journal of yours and brainstorm your biggest passions – the things that *really* get you going. Maybe that love of texture and beadwork is actually transference from a painting hobby put on the back-burner. Perhaps you adore salsa dancing, baking tarts and cakes, trimming bonsai, hill walking – hell, maybe you've got a thing for ironing (there's always one).

In other words, if you shop to fill a void, think of the other ways you can replenish your emotional reserves. Controlling that trigger finger requires consistency, so start crafting regular time in your week, however small, dedicated to your well-being. Make sure it's something you connect with, have done before and can easily reactivate, rather than exhausting mental focus on starting something new.

Habits are like mean girls – they rule the school, but with some healthy competition, focus can easily be shifted to a cooler clique. Nevertheless, all it takes is an offer to sit together at lunch for a moment of weakness to take hold. Being actively aware of your potential trip-wire means you're less likely to repeat the action that causes you pain, especially if there's an alternative. What's more, you'll never again have to wear pink on Wednesdays.

CHAPTER THREE

HOW WE SHOP AND WHY WE HOARD

THE FEMALE PSYCHE

THE FEMALE PSYCHE

'I've taken over the guest room wardrobe too – plus, I've
arranged all my shoes on the bookshelves on the landing.
(I put the books in boxes. No one ever read them anyway.)'

SOPHIE KINSELLA, *MINI SHOPAHOLIC*

When *Sex and the City: The Movie* was released in
2007, fans across the world heaved a collective
sigh as Mr Big showed Carrie her new walk-in
wardrobe. These audible gasps had little to do
with its frosted glass doors, etched art deco patterning or hand-
bevelled mirrored glass, and more to do with its palatial sense
of space – a new wardrobe frontier just waiting to be filled.
Square footage, as most Manhattanites will attest, is a covetable
commodity. Mr Big's ability to hunt down the perfect Park
Avenue wardrobe not only fed into Carrie's legendary gathering
tendencies but eliminated any turf wars resulting from a shared
closet. For movie-goers, the empty space tapped into a deep-
rooted territorial psyche, prompting delicious fantasies of how
we'd furnish our own kingdoms. Whether filled with M&S or
Manolo Blahnik, the need to 'name it and claim it' is more than
a superficial pursuit – it is an evolutionary compulsion that
reinforces our individual sense of identity.

According to evolutionary psychology, this stashing urge, in fact, has its roots in Neolithic tribes who hunted and gathered for sustenance. Commonly, men hunted for big game, which involved physical strength, a knack for spatial geometry and a singular approach to getting the kill. Women, on the other hand, gathered fruit and vegetables together in groups. This involved remembering where foodstuffs were located or hidden and determining their value through colour and shape, touch and feel. This, consumer studies maintain, has evolved over time and adapted to fit the modern milieu of the retail jungle, in which women exhibit similar skills: the ability to examine, compare and collect over many hours in the company of friends – with the added benefit of a Starbucks refuel. You see, it's all your ancestors' fault. Well, maybe not.

Before you blame that wardrobe-avalanche waiting to happen on some prehistoric gender bias, it is best to clarify a few things. Women know how to hunt and, damn, can they do it well. Whether it's queuing from 5 a.m. on Black Friday for a Burberry bag, pre-ordering those filigree sunglasses online or grabbing armfuls of designer cast-offs at a heaving sample sale, females are predominantly alpha-hunters, conquering with credit cards and wearing their kill with pride.

In that span of 10,000 years or so, a little bugbear called consumerist culture developed, throwing a proverbial spanner in the works. Feeding your shopping habit cannot justifiably be compared with feeding a family of hair-shirted neoliths. Then again, *Homo erectus* didn't have savvy marketers pressing her emotional buttons with buzzwords like 'must-have' and '3 for 2' – but more about that later.

With the advent of the retail jungle, our prehistoric survival instinct has become more non-essential and, as such, self-motivated. We've moved away from the tribe and have instead formed tribal allegiances with shops and brands, viewing retail as a reward rather than a reason. Increasingly, the lines between 'want' and 'need' have become decidedly blurred. All of a sudden, buying a top in ten colours seems a perfectly rational idea – and who doesn't need a titanium-plated Bluetooth necklace? This kind of excess creates extra weight – the kind that bogs you down both physically and psychologically. And yet we persist, hooked on the emotional release from our desired reward: the heady cocktail of endorphins that keeps us riding the retail high. It's not as if shops only want you to visit once. So just what causes this rinse-and-repeat behaviour?

THE PSYCHOLOGY OF SHOPPING

'The quickest way to know a woman is to go shopping with her.'

MARCELENE COX

Darwin's theory of evolution: it's not the first thing that

springs to mind when indulging in retail therapy. That said, the survival of the fittest is the precise lodestone which underpins our buying behaviour, making us buy things we don't need – or even want. Think of yourself as a considered shopper? Think again.

We may not be rocking this season's loincloth but our hereditary herd instinct hasn't left us – it's just been redirected. Like many evolutionary coping mechanisms (I'm looking at you, Mr Basal Ganglia!), group mentality may have been a viable survival strategy against prehistoric predators but over time we've outgrown its use.

Physical threats of yore (not eating; being eaten) have morphed into equally imminent emotional fears with perceived social exclusion (the equivalent of being mauled by a sabre-toothed cat) keeping shoppers primed at all times.

Not so kindly, today's style stragglers are referred to as 'late adapters'; back in the day, they would've been called 'dinner'. You get the picture. Aversion to loss is more than just a free-form fear – it is central to natural selection. Combine this ancestral predilection with a dollop of stress and an itch for instant gratification and waddayaknow, we've got ourselves one hot mess.

Flash sales, limited-edition merchandise, calls-to-action, for-one-day-only promotions, newsletter nudges and exclusive offerings all tap into our fashion FoMo (Fear of Missing out) – the angst of being absent from the rewards enjoyed by others.

And let's be honest: no one likes missing out. Community and social bonding underpin our most basic human instincts, which makes being left to pasture a bit of a bummer. Retailers have cleverly tapped into this deep-seated anxiety, playing on FoMo's infamous sidekick – regret. You either nail that sale or go home empty-handed, tackle that trend or live with being 'last season'.

It's 'do or die' – even though death holds no dominion over missing out on the latest designer–high street collaboration. The result? Cold facts get the cold shoulder as stress levels rise and we are led by the proverbial pants.

Admittedly, nothing feels quite like bagging some swag: the rush of pheromones to the brain, the seeming validation of your fiscal prowess, the tales of heroic sale slaying, the parading of your retail kill. Equally, nothing feels quite like feeling special: opening a 'Just for You!' email from your favourite shop, being tagged in a 'Lust List' tweet, sneaking off to a private trunk-show – that's enough to get the heart racing and the wallet lubricated, dontcha think?

Rolf Dobelli, author of *The Art of Thinking Clearly*, refers to this phenomenon as the 'Scarcity Error', where rare is seen as valuable (even if it is worth nothing). Conditional phrases beginning with 'only' ('only while stocks last', 'only today', 'only online') cause shoppers to see a prospect in short supply – and act as a panic button to trigger a classic feeding frenzy. Moreover, the idea of being left in the fashion tundra flies in the face of our evolutionary competitive streak. Credit and store card interest rates, next-day delivery surcharges: all of these conspire to exploit our animal instinct – the 'must-have' mentality that has our wardrobes filled with fads, fluff and foolish mistakes.

Our desire for immediacy and its attendant gratification is what has us in the notorious 'wardrobe full of clothes and nothing to wear' quandary. 'The closer a reward is, the higher our "emotional interest rate" rises and the more we are willing to give in exchange for it,' says Dobelli. The more instant a reward, the less willing we are to postpone its delicious thrill.

Psychologists refer to this as 'bounded rationality'. In other words, we have self-control until such time as we really need it. It's when faced with the object of our desires that the brain shifts into reward-seeking fifth gear to make sure we don't miss out. But when the buzz wears off and the pink fairy dust has settled, we begin to see things a little differently. Was that pair of drop-crotch harem trousers worth the splurge? Did you actually 'need it now', like the website said? Is that ra-ra skirt really 'to die for' or is it actually a bit *meh*? More to the point, are you willing to admit it or do you prefer to rationalise your dodgy decisions?

This is not a wrist-slapping exercise by any means. We all have a story to tell. My own include: that red leather jacket I insisted was off-duty model material rather than that of a Michael Jackson 'Thriller' tribute; those too-tight T-bar sandals that squeezed my feet like a fistful of Play Doh; and not forgetting the curiously draped dress that took a degree in engineering and an act of God to remove. *I slept in it once out of sheer despair.* Rather than admit defeat, I carefully crafted a rather spurious explanation – to myself and others – as to why I insisted on wearing them:

'80s zombie chic is back … I can feel it.

I deliberately bought them this size. They'll loosen up with a bit of wear.

It's a dress AND a brain puzzle. Who knew?

Psychologists call this anomaly 'confirmation bias': having to reconcile a sub-par purchase in order to safeguard the integrity of one's judgement. The fact is, most of us buy on emotion. It is only with hindsight that we look to reinterpret the evidence, reshaping it to foreclose on the brain's flub and show we were right all along.

It's official – logic has left the building. Busted. So how do you get it back?

ARE YOU EMOTIONAL OR UNCONSCIOUS? TACKLING YOUR SHOPPING TYPE

'What are they doing? Why do they come here?'
'Some kind of instinct. Memory of what they used to do.
This was an important place in their lives.'

DAWN OF THE DEAD

Ever wonder why zombies gravitate towards shopping centres? Really – think about it. It's the apocalypse. Things are pretty calamitous, as you would expect at The End of Time – yet the undead feel compelled to get their shop on. Worse still are those who choose to hide from said stalkers *inside* the centres. Ask anyone: that shop layout is meant to keep you there, not help you escape. *Didn't exactly think that one through now, did you, sunshine?*

Not surprisingly, today's shopper shares a few commonalities with these catatonic creatures, including but not limited to the following:

a) A craving for consumption (brain-eating or retail, take your pick)

b) A force of habit

c) A will external to one's own

Sure, you may be in agreement with points a) and b), minus the cranial caviar, but you've probably raised a suspicious eyebrow to c). I mean, we're arbiters of our own free will, after all. We're in control; we know what we want. We're nobody's slaves.

Hate to break it to you, but we don't always know what we're doing. Scary, isn't it? We may be groomed in the habit of shopping, but as self-determined beings, we do like to think we've got some say in how we shop and what we buy. Well, not so much. Death and destruction notwithstanding, our cannibalistic cohorts instinctively gravitated to the shopping centre as was their habit as humans. So established and routine was this behaviour in their past, it continued to mindlessly drive their present, unknown even to them.

Much in the same way, our shopping habits often reside outside the parameters of free will.

Consider this:

- How many times have you gone to buy toothpaste and hairspray and come home with a new dress/necklace/feather boa/ski jacket/complete ballroom dancing ensemble (delete as appropriate)?
- How many times have you managed to justify said purchase to yourself/your partner/your family/your friends/your bank manager/your cat (delete as appropriate)?

- How many times have you stumbled across said purchase
  only to ask yourself when/where/why/how did I buy this
  (delete as appropriate)? No recollection, nada, none.

Truth be told, conscious will is a bit of a farce. The sooner we raise our awareness of this fact, the easier it will be to create happier closets. The late American social psychologist Daniel M. Wegner said it best: 'When life creates all the inevitable situations in which we find ourselves acting without appropriate prior conscious thoughts, we must protect the illusion of conscious will by trying to make sense of our actions.'

In other words, our conscious minds are sneaky feckers, making excuses for our poor unconscious choices and, quite often, hiding the evidence. Out of sight, out of mind – literally.

Not all our true motives for our purchases are hidden. Sometimes we're led by desire – pure and simple. There are, in fact, three key drivers, aside from need, that pique a purchase: celebration, compensation and gratification. Personal accomplishments like weight loss or a promotion give cause for celebration, while compensation acts as a salve for disappointments like a break-up or a case of the blues. Gratification is shopping for the pleasure of it.

None of these in and of themselves is cause for concern (why else would they call it retail therapy?). Nevertheless, it is important to connect with our emotions rather than be dictated to by them.

Think about it:

- How often have you felt unique/special/treated because of a special offer/customer invitation/loyalty card points?
- How often have you felt in control/smug/bad-ass at having clocked a lesser-spotted sale (needed or otherwise)?
- How often have you felt close to orgasm/selling a kidney/selling your soul at the sight of something new in your favourite shop?
- How often have you felt guilty about the amount you buy and/or don't wear?
- How often have you felt stressed/anxious/irritated by sheer choice and either bought an item you didn't want or went home with nothing?

More than you care to admit? Yep, me too. Truth be told, we are all emotional shoppers. According to Kit Yarrow, author of *Decoding the New Consumer Mind,* our technocratic culture and its access to instant information has only intensified this reaction to shopping. 'Interruption-driven, overstimulated, distracted consumers have less ability to focus and less conscious brain space available to make decisions.' The super-saturation of offers, both online and in real time, has decreased our attention span, says Yarrow, and, in turn, has affected our ability to discern the intrinsic value of what we're buying. It's shopping, Jim, but not as we know it. And the fact is – we don't. But all is not lost. Not by a long shot. The fact is, retail *is* therapeutic and has the enormous power to mollify our mood – both short- and long-term. The trick is in harnessing those emotions in a more meaningful, less fear-based way. In a world beset by interminable alternatives, being mindful of what you want and why you want it is easier said than done. That's why you're going to make a To Don't List: a manifesto of what you can't wear, shouldn't buy and won't consider.

THE TO DON'T LIST

There's a beautifully backwards logic to the To Don't List. Unlike to do lists that pretty much set you up for a fail (how often do you actually do what you have to do?), reversing the process creates less pressure and thus more flow.

This is what James Clear refers to as a 'Bright-Line' Rule – a clearly defined rule with little wiggle room that can be used to break bad habits and build new identity-based behaviours. The Plastics did it (to less generous effect) in *Mean Girls* with their Draconian dress code: coloured shoes on Monday, slogan tees on Tuesday, the infamous pink on Wednesdays.

A more positive bright-line rule can be applied by ruling out what you don't wear. In saying what you *don't* as opposed to *can't* wear, the bright-line rule flips the script from self-sacrifice to self-empowerment. What's more, as Clear points out in his blog, it turbo-boosts our willpower by alleviating decision fatigue. Break the list into the following sections:

- Colours
- Shapes
- Styles
- Trends

Be specific and, more important, be honest. No point wearing a polo neck if you look like you're being suffocated by a knitted guillotine. If calf-width and knee boots conspire to restrict your blood supply, then do the decent thing and go ankle-length.

Establishing boundaries means knowing your limits. Not sure what suits you? Tune into your feelings. If it doesn't make you want a private moment in the dressing room, then it's probably not a keeper. If you don't feel good in it, you won't look good in it. If you don't look forward to the next time you wear it, you won't wear it again. Simple as.

I'll start us off. It's always me, isn't it?

Cut/Style	Why?	Replace with
Skinny leg	My thighs resemble over-stuffed sausages.	Straight-cut or skinny flare/bootcut to balance my hips
Crew neck	I have a uni-boob or something resembling the Continental Shelf.	A low scoop or V-neck
Cut-off denim shorts	I look like I should be charging by the hour.	City shorts or culottes
Super high heels	I walk like a demented baby giraffe.	Mid-heel, cool flat or easy-to-wear wedge
High-rise/ low-rise	My arse looks like a rectangle. Two words: builder's crack.	Flattering mid-rise that covers my decency but gives me a pert bum

Colour/Trend	Why?	Replace with
Mustard yellow	I look jaundiced or like '70s wallpaper.	Golden yellow – lighter and brighter
Grey	I look like a corpse.	Navy blue – much kinder on my skin tone
Granny chic	I look like I escaped from a knitting convention or the local bridge club.	Shapely styles that highlight my figure
Boho	I look like the president of the local Grateful Dead chapter.	Tailored grown-up styles that look less like a flower child
Jumpsuits	I look like a convict or a bin man.	Trousers and a top – avoid the adult onesie at all costs

It's only by committing to what you won't (or simply can't) wear that you are free to explore other, more fulfilling alternatives that don't involve carpal tunnel syndrome or a trip to A&E. As restrictive as this exercise may sound, there's a certain alchemy to it. Sift away the base metals of your wardrobe and you'll soon find the gold – the core clothing values that make getting dressed a ritual rather than a routine.

Sure, the odd impulse buy never hurt anyone and a few cheap and cheerful numbers won't cause total closet calamity; but the more you give yourself permission (see Chapter 2, 'Excuses, Excuses, Excuses'), the quicker those one-offs become hardcore habits.

So how do you navigate the myriad of tissue-wrapped distractions and stay true to your sartorial identity? It's a question of learning the 'trouble entendre': the silver-tongued speech that loosens your purse strings and has you sorely regretting that fast fashion fling.

HOW TO SPEAK RETAIL

'Give them what they never knew they wanted.'

DIANA VREELAND

Language is the master manipulator. All it takes is a few well-placed words to convince you that a dress you'll never wear is worth buying. How? By divorcing decision from intent and using highly emotive vocabulary to tap into the right side of the brain – the seat of suggestion, the palace of persuasion.

When it comes to sales and marketing, persuasion *always* arrives in its best suit, Don Draper style – handsome and unthreatening, charismatic and clean cut. Persuasion wants to help you get the best deals, to give you the inside track, to treat yourself to something nice. So you feel comfortable around persuasion, right? After all, he's got your back. But persuasion doesn't want you to get *too* comfortable. After all, he's got a job to do and that's getting you to pony up and put out. He takes all major credit cards, by the way, and PayPal and sometimes, if he's feeling generous, he'll even spread out your payments over a few months. That's just the way he is. Or is it? Don't fall for the charm offensive – this guy is a peerless player with more tricks up his French-cuffed sleeve than Penn and Teller. He doesn't just know how to play the game; he damn well invented it. Here's how to spot the ultimate pick-up artist in action.

Connect: He'll make you feel special. Really special. In fact, he sees you as a champion (his brand champion, that is). Don't be fooled by his private perks or any special discounts he claims are 'just for you' – he says that to all the girls.

Control: Him? Slippery? Never. He'll make you think you're in charge of the interaction by using words like 'select', 'choose', 'master' and 'experience'. You choose. Or do you?

Confidential: He'll let you in on a little secret. He normally doesn't tell people this but you're different. You strike him as the kind of person who makes good decisions, so he reckons you'll love this insider tip – 40% off your next purchase and free shipping and returns (not that you'll need it) if you sign up today and spend at least €250. Now that's a deal.

Compel: He may make you think you're in control of the relationship but there's always a condition to his overtures, urging you to take action before it's too late. (Sexual tension, much?) Offer ends at midnight! Sale must end now! Get it or regret it. And we don't like regret, now do we?

Covetable: Don't believe he's a catch? Watch him sell it with a zealot: big-time bloggers singing his praises; celebrity endorsements; a Facebook fan page of happy shoppers bonding over shared 'experiences'. If that's not social proof, I don't know what is …

Condition: Did he tell you about this amazing deal? You know, the deal that's amazing. Amazingly, he thought he did because it's such a deal. Dealing with so many people, sometimes he doesn't always remember, which is ironic because the subconscious responds so well to repetition. Amazing how the brain works, isn't it?

Conversion: Once he's worked his game, he's got you in the palm of his hand or rather vice versa. So are you going to show me what's in that bag you're carrying?

Cracking the Code

Anyone who's ever toyed with a foreign language understands the complexities of translation. I once ordered a donkey instead of butter in a Spanish bakery, while my friend (the bigger ass) discovered that grapefruit and a certain sexual act sound incriminatingly similar in Italian. Let's just say he won't be returning to that supermarket again. Retail lingo, although ostensibly clear, bears its own set of subtexts and nuances. Ever left a shop with something you weren't planning on buying? Who hasn't? The trick is to crack the code so that buying is done on your terms – not someone's sales targets. Prepare for a crash course in shop speak ...

Hello! = I see you. Don't try and hide.

It really suits you. = I'm on commission.

You look ah-*mazing*! = I haven't made my targets this month.

They're supposed to fit that way. = Couldn't flog these with a dungeon of whips and chains.

You'll get so much wear out of that. = You'll wear it once and it'll never see the light of day again.

You're supposed to wear it with this top. = Let me sell you something else you don't need.

They'll start to loosen with wear. = How do you feel about amputation?

That's the last one. = We don't have your size.

This is our best seller. = You look unsure about this neon fishnet
mini-skirt. Let me pitch it to you.

Would you like to sign up to our mailing list? = Sucker! We've got
you now!

It's limited edition. = It's very expensive.

I have the same pair! = My manager is watching …

Do you want to try that on? = Are you buying that?

I'll just grab you a changing room. = Let's get this sale rolling.

Do you need shoes with that? = Everyone looks better in heels.

How are you doing in the changing room? = Why are you taking
so long?

How did you get on? = Seriously, are you buying that?

Are you interested in signing up for our loyalty card? = You seem
loose with the purse strings. Can I get you to buy more?

It's a huge trend this season. = It's got a shelf-life of a month.

We just sold three of these today. = You'll look like everyone else.

Call-to-Action

Definition: A marketing instruction designed to provoke an
immediate, knee-jerk response, usually involving an imperative
verb and short timeframe. Most successfully used in email
format. Also known as 'allowing your buttons to be pressed'.

Think of it: if it's true that 66% of us have purchased
something on the basis of an email entreaty, then going online
requires a metric tonne of conscious awareness. Given that

you've already shared your online browsing patterns by clicking on the 'OK to cookies' button (these are not the chocolate chip variety), not to mention your purchase history by redeeming your loyalty card points (conversion comes at a price), then it's no surprise that you feel called to act. They've given you what you didn't even know you wanted. Clever.

Going going GONE!

Get it before it's gone!

Get in on the action before it's too late!

Get it or regret it!

Get it now!

EXCLAMATION MARKS!!!

Yes. This is for real!

Today only!

This week only!

This weekend only!

The day after tomorrow only!

10% off everything. Ends midnight!

Quick – 20% off jackets and coats. Offer ends Monday.

Take an extra 30% off – buy now, wear now styles.

Hurry. Free express shipping ends tomorrow.

Free express shipping ends tomorrow on all orders over €300.

Hurry, offer must end …

Seriously, what's the issue? Get moving!

Sign up now.   Unlimited next-day delivery for a year.

Shop now!

Easy ways to pay.

Not to be missed.

Spend €175 to get free express delivery.

Join now for up to €70 free credit.

Don't be the last to know!

Don't miss out!

Don't miss out on your dream buy!

Don't delay!

Don't delay your dream buy!

MORE EXCLAMATION MARKS!!!!!

Stay one step ahead.

Why wait?

Really, why are you waiting?

Treat yourself.

You deserve it.

Up to 70% hot new lines. Every. Single. Day.

Always up to 60% off. Yes, really.

One more chance to buy.

Last chance to buy!

You can't afford to miss this!

Buy now, wear now.

Buy now, regret never.

Go on. You know you want it!

Go on, go on, go on.

Be the first to find out.

Shop the front row.

Shop the shoot.

Shop the must-have now or else edit.

Shop like a stylist.

Shop like a blogger.

Shop like an editor.

Shop like a maniac.

Shop. Just bloody shop …

Sweet Nothings

Mastering shop speak is one thing; circumnavigating magazine jargon, snazzy ad speak and anything that makes its way into your inbox or smartphone is quite another. Just when you think you've controlled your urge to splurge, an arousing, urgent and hedonic headline grabs your attention and gives it a good spanking. Oh, I say! Eager for some more, you allow yourself to be seduced by the dirty talk. And like a lot of filthy promises, the fantasy is the star of the show. Before you know it, you've bought a pink feather bolero that makes you look like a Miami Beach flamingo – lesser-spotted and with good reason. You feel let down, crestfallen and, truth be told, slightly frustrated but you're too embarrassed to ask for a refund because you believed you'd be dazzled. You were prepared to be blown away – much like the last time and the time before. The promises, oh, the promises. Don't be fooled. It's a honey trap!

Your winter wardrobe sorted

We've got you sorted

Dresses decoded

Trousers translated

Sweaters simplified

The new bag lexicon

Master new season style

24/7 style dilemmas solved

Instant outfit updates

Accessories alert

COMING SOON!

Weekly most wanted

Your dream dress is waiting

Prepare to be inspired

Prepare to be dazzled

Prepare to be obsessed

Style stalking!

Ponchos are actually back.

Patchwork ponchos are really
    back. Honest.

#want

#need

#I.Die

We love: make it mine

We want it all

Trending now

How to dress up now

How to stand out

New season now

New season … New bag!

Tackle the new season

Own the new season

P*wn the new season

Buy now, wear now

The look of now	We're coveting
The key pieces now	We're crushing on
Need to know now	We're loving
So now	We're all over it
So very now	From us to you
Now. Just now.	Just for you
The Lust List	All for you
We're feeling it	For you

PURGING THE URGE TO SPLURGE

Urge

noun: an involuntary, natural or instinctive impulse.

Having an urge is always sudden and most pass without attention, with the exception of bodily functions, which, if not attended to immediately, can have embarrassing and/or potentially disastrous consequences. 'Don't hold it in!' as your mother used to tell your 3-year old self when doing the pee-pee dance. But when it comes to spending like a Russian oligarch after a few White Russians, the pee-pee dance is perfectly acceptable (unless you've actually had a few cocktails – then you might want to visit the ladies' room). As mentioned in Chapter 2, willpower is self-regulating and is sustained only by equal amounts of effort and desire. Want to dial down the thrill of the till? Check out the happiness hacks below.

HAPPINESS HACKS

Keep focused: Do NOT answer your phone, check emails or social media while shopping. Seriously. Wait for that coffee break instead. Any contextual switch requires an equivalent mental gear shift. Too many of these and the recovery process placed on the brain can delay getting back into focus by up to 25 minutes, which affects the ability to make decent decisions. Think of how many times you've pulled the old switcheroo today. If energy flows where attention goes, then consider it a form of mindful time management.

Good for: All closet types

Think beyond the moment: Consider how what you are buying fits into your bigger closet picture. The effect of the word 'now' on shoppers has been proved to short-circuit the brain's valuation process. *(Remember: anything that is referred to as 'now' becomes 'then' just as quickly.)* Equally, sales have an inimitable way of making us stock up on items we'd never have bought in the first place. The cult of now, reinforced by the proliferation of resale and auction websites, has created an interim attitude to clothing and has, in effect, reformatted how we view our wardrobes. Why bother assessing the true worth of a garment or its cost-per-wear ratio (CPW = price ÷ estimated amount of wears) if we can always sell it? That said, high-yield pieces can deliver a canny return on investment. More on that in Chapter 10 . . .

Good for: Impulse Buyer, Split Personality, Sale Sniper

You're not that special: Here's the thing. The VIP customer invite you received the other day? Six hundred other people received one too. Oh, and that platinum upgrade on your shop loyalty card is only because you spend so much ... and they want you to spend more. And no, you don't deserve another pair of shoes; you already have 80. Now, take off those rose-tinted glasses and take your ego for a stiff drink. *Ouch, that had to hurt.*

Good for: Impulse Buyer, Split Personality, Sale Sniper

Go with your gut: Got that familiar feeling? Yes, we've all been there. You could have sworn there was steam coming from the ATM last you used it and your heavily pregnant credit card is fit to buckle under the weight of a hefty bank charge – yet you still raised your virtual paddle to bid on those knee-high Grecian sandals. Now you've got an acute case of the guilt sweats. You could cover your hands in cling film, spray yourself with Teflon or hire an assistant to Taser you in moments of weakness. Or you could simply go with your gut. If it doesn't feel good inside, it's not worth what it looks like on the outside.

Good for: Impulse Buyer, Secret Shopper, Split Personality

Delay gratification: Postponing pleasure may seem draconian but, ironically, it serves to increase long-term happiness. Feeling tempted? Neuroscience studies prove that when dopamine tickles the brain's pleasure receptors, it can take a full 30 minutes to recover. The only way is to walk away.

Use bargaining tools (much like we do with children) to help dampen the desire. Tell yourself you can buy it tomorrow. When tomorrow comes, check in with how you feel. This will allow time for your brain to figure out whether this is a need or simply a want that can wait.

Good for: Impulse Buyer, Secret Shopper, Split Personality, Sale Sniper

Discover your personal discount rate: Our self-control can get put through the wringer unless we are aware of our personal discount rate. And no, I'm not talking about store cards or that extra 10% off at the till you get when the manager isn't around. I'm talking about the measure of your happiness now versus that of tomorrow. In other words, what are you willing to sacrifice to get what you want? Are you willing to forego this season's crochet knit shorts now so that you can go on that family holiday later? If in doubt, ask your future self which she'd regret not having had. Remember: we only rue the days that didn't bring us happiness, and memories are rarely for sale.

Good for: Impulse Buyer, Secret Shopper, Split Personality, Sale Sniper

Pay and display: Stick receipts where you can see them: on the mirror, on the fridge door, by the kettle – whatever you use most on a daily basis. A visual reminder keeps us tethered to reality when the fantasy fairy comes-a-knocking. Add them up each week and see what exactly you are spending your hard-earned cash on. It might be the wake-up call you need.

Good for: Secret Shopper, Sale Sniper

Name it and shame it: So the dog ate your receipts, did he? That happens. But did you hear of a site called DogShaming.com? You post a pic of the damage done by your pesky pup with a sign hanging around his fuzzy little neck by way of public humiliation. It's kind of cute – and addictive. Not to get off topic but how about we do the same with you? Come on, it'll be fun! I'll cover you in a ticker tape of receipts and we can post the evidence on Instagram, Twitter and Facebook. Then let's crowdsource the most damning comments and you can recite them in moments of future weakness. #hoarder #didispendthismuch? #dontjudge #golddigger

Good for: Impulse Buyer, Secret Shopper, Split Personality, Sale Sniper

Dodge the danger zones: Are there any times of the day or situations when you are more likely to shop? Do you browse on your lunch break? Have a nose on the way home from work? Identify the danger zones and implement an alternative strategy: read a book; take a different route home. Commit to doing something different until the impulse has passed or, ideally, until the new behaviour becomes habit.

Good for: Impulse Buyer, Secret Shopper, Split Personality, Sale Sniper

Plan it, dammit: Schedule your shopping for a month on a need-to-do basis and see how you manage. Remember the components of willpower: will and power. You've got to want to make it work and that involves taking control. Got a Saturday shopping ritual? Swap that out for a competing response like exercising, which fires up our endorphins much in the same way as a spot of retail therapy. Can't log on without clicking to cart? Block your favourite shopping websites for a month. It is proved scientifically that when rewards are visible, they become harder to resist, so work with your willpower – not against it. Most important, don't forget to diarise your shopping diet daily. It's only in managing a habit that we realise how much time we spent (or wasted) on cultivating it in the first place.

Good for: Impulse Buyer, Split Personality, Sale Sniper

Seeing is believing: Don't hide your haul. Much like credit cards, stashing creates a deferred reality between what we buy and what we admit to having bought. Taking stock of your closet collateral leads to a more revealing emotional inventory by confronting the underlying behaviour. Start by removing every item in bags and boxes from inside your wardrobe. Place each item around the room where they are clearly visible and photograph the evidence. Use this as your phone screensaver or post the evidence on social media. Every time you get tempted by some new loot, look at what you already have and ask yourself 'Why?'

Good for: Secret Shopper, Sale Sniper

Touching, isn't it?: Consumer studies have proved that shoppers form emotional bonds with things they touch or hold. The longer the physical contact, the higher value and perceived ownership we assign to that object. According to Paco Underhill, author of the best-selling tome *Why We Buy: The Science of Shopping*, shoppers are twice as likely to buy a garment once they've tried it on. Think of that the next time someone tries hustling you into a changing room!

Good for: All closet types

Change your mind: That dress would look so amazing on you, wouldn't it? What if I told you 150 people had already tried it on and that it was rife with dead skin cells, sweat, make-up stains and thong sweat? Not so appealing now, is it? According to leading psychologist (and the main man behind the infamous Stanford marshmallow test, a series of studies on delayed gratification) Walter Mischel, the power lies not in the object of your desire but in how it is mentally evaluated. Hot temptations become radically cooled with a few terrible mental images, which, in turn, have the capacity to impact on our feelings when faced with temptation.

Good for: Impulse Buyer, Split Personality, Sale Sniper

Craft a contingency plan: Walking past a sale sign isn't easy – fact. The brash font, the bold typography, the colour red – all combine to excite the brain's fight-or-flight response, speeding up the metabolism and causing faster breathing. Combine this with a heaping dose of fashion FoMo and Houston, we've got ourselves a problem. Fear of missing out (aka loss aversion) is so hardwired that it can often overpower our fear of making a bad choice, even if that means having to put up with the yenting voice of regret. In such cases, Walter Mischel suggests the If–Then contingency plan. In other words, by identifying what triggers our impulses, we can implement a strategy to keep them under control – for example: 'If I see a sale sign, I'm going to remind myself that I am €3,000 in credit card debt'. By anticipating a likely scenario, the conscious mind knows to sound the alarm the moment it happens.

Good for: Impulse Buyer, Split Personality, Sale Sniper

In need of more persuasion? Then read on for an eye-opening lesson on the effect of options on our brain and excess on our hearts. Whatever you do, don't sit on the fence – *it leaves marks …*

CHAPTER FOUR

LESS IS MORE — WHY WE DON'T ACTUALLY NEED THAT STUFF

THE PARADOX OF CHOICE

'When faced with two equally tough choices, most people choose the third choice: to not choose.'

JAROD KINTZ, *THE BOOK TITLE IS INVISIBLE*

I magine the following scenario. You decide to go jeans shopping and discover an epic denim bar with its own menu of cuts, washes, lengths and colours. A sales assistant sporting Buddy Holly glasses and unending confidence asks you if you need help. Of course you do, but you tell her you're just looking. After all, it can't be that difficult. You scan hundreds upon hundreds of pairs all meticulously labelled and categorised according to their unique selling points. Suddenly, what seems like a simple exercise starts to feel as logical as advanced calculus with a hangover. Brain freeze dictates a swift exit, so you head home, plug in and continue your mission online. Only this time, the square root of pi has multiplied to include a host of countless variables. Now you can either look like a high-rise extreme-distressed mom or a slim bleached boyfriend with busted knees – your pick. So you don't. You've got a pair of leggings in the house somewhere – that ought to do.

Choice: it's a bit like salt. Small doses add flavour; anything more and you're looking at high blood pressure. Too many options create anxiety and, in turn, weaken our decision muscle. The result? We either snuggle up to the security blanket of stuff or suffer option paralysis – fearful, in both cases, of choosing poorly.

American psychologist Barry Schwartz, author of *The Paradox of Choice: Why More Is Less,* maintains that making rational decisions is next to impossible when endless opportunity clutters the mind – a modern malady known as 'option paralysis'. The greater the variety, the less sure we are of our selection and, as outlined in Chapter 3, we all like to think we know what we're doing. Having a menu is one thing; having the Magna Carta is quite another.

And here's the kicker. For all the Impulse Buyers, Doomsday Preppers and Split Personalities who gravitate towards volume and newness, there is an equal number of shoppers who are effectively blinded by their presence. This psychological quirk, known as 'reflexive mental processing', causes shoppers to manage choice (and regret) by unconsciously screening out the new and unfamiliar.

Picture it: you go shopping on the same day and in the same shop as a friend but while you come home with another white T-shirt, she manages to snag a pair of killer trousers you never even saw. That's right. The basal ganglia are back in a bid to exert quality control over the vast amount of data the mind has to process. And what better way to screen out the unfamiliar than by focusing on existing connections: the easy, the routine, the old reliable.

There's a good reason we refer to ourselves as 'creatures of habit'. On occasion we'll go balls to the wall and bust out of our comfort zone but generally we revert to a style default. Often this default, be it a wiggle-worthy pencil skirt or an easy sweatshirt, has an emotional tether to a compliment, a feeling (youthful, maternal, powerful) or a state of being (nostalgic, safe), which makes it all the more compelling and thus trickier to challenge.

And let's be honest: the brain is a bit of a wuss and does its level best to avoid any psychological discomfort. What's more, the basal ganglia, being typical Jenny Jobsworths, want to save the brain time and effort in making decisions, which, in turn, makes us feel capable and competent.

Sometimes, the mental energy required to investigate the new just isn't worth the slog. The fact is, the older we get, the more habit-prone and thus predictable we become. In the words of Jeremy Dean, 'Habit provides a safety zone, but it's also a kind of cage from which escape is hard.' So unless you're under 5 years old or are Linus van Pelt, it's best you put the kibosh on that sartorial safety blanket and prepare to usher in some new habits.

Do you know your denim?

Straight

Bootcut

Slight bootcut

Flare

Skinny flare

Cropped

Capri

Slim

Skinny

Relaxed skinny

Contour skinny

Second-skin skinny

Super-skinny

Ultra-skinny

Power-skinny

Turbo-skinny

Spray-on

Jeggings

Rip-knee

Displaced rip-knee

Thigh-rip

Extreme thigh-rip

Distressed

Bleached

Acid-wash

Snow-wash

Vintage-wash

Mid-wash

Light wash

Dark wash

Stone-wash

Boyfriend

Girlfriend

Mom

Slim mom

Slim mom with busted knees

Extreme-distressed slim mom
   with busted knees

High-rise extreme-distressed
   slim mom with busted
   knees and thigh rips

Four-way stretch

Super-stretch

Power-stretch

Mid-rise

Low-rise

High-rise

Bum-lifters

Hip-huggers

Ankle-grazers

Whiskers

Patchwork

Jet-pocket

Four-pocket

Five-pocket

Button-fly

Zip fly

No fly

Oh my …

FASHION BINGO

Suffering from fashion overwhelm? Can't understand why there are so many bloody dresses? This little exercise demonstrates what happens to logic when a surfeit of choice bullies its way into the equation. Want to play? Close your eyes and choose the following items from the table below at random: one fabric, two details, one style and one print. Bingo: You've got yourself a dress! A ruffled drop-waist holographic paisley sundress. Told you choice was a bit of a harridan.

Fabric	Detail	Style	Print
neoprene	drop-waist	maxi	Liberty
sequin	cold shoulder	midi	gingham
holographic	high-low hem	mini	floral
crepe	off-the-shoulder	skater	check
silk	tie-waist	shirt	stripe
organza	halter neck	sweater	polka dot
wool	bandeau	shift	paisley
corduroy	peplum	swing	graphic
leather	sleeveless	smock	painterly
satin	draped	slip	colour block
cashmere	peek-a-boo	bodycon	novelty
chiffon	pleated	ballgown	leopard
tapestry	fringe	tunic	reptile
cotton	plunge neck	T-shirt	tropical
jacquard	drop hem	wrap	Aztec
tweed	asymmetric	wiggle	scarf
houndstooth	polo neck	pinafore	abstract
suede	one-shoulder	prom	pinstripe
jersey	backless	kimono	geo
patent leather	embroidered	sundress	fable
disco lamé	cowl neck	tea dress	watercolour
polyester	ruffled	bandage	Pendleton
lace	button front	fit-and-flare	tie-dye
fishnet	panelled	beach	feather
linen	laser-cut	gypsy	vintage
tulle	scalloped	Grecian	marble
fur	appliqué	pencil	chinoiserie
broderie	batwing	cocktail	Dalmatian
velvet	bubble hem	A-line	batik
crochet	strappy	babydoll	
quilted	slit front	muumuu	
mesh	flute sleeve	tent	

SECURITY BLANKETS ARE FOR KIDS

'But the more we amass – the more we need our stockpile – the more uncertain we feel … Real security, however, is found inside us, in consistent personal growth, not in reliance on external factors.'

THE MINIMALISTS, *EVERYTHING THAT REMAINS*

Security is defined as freedom from concern, anxiety or doubt. Ironically, the very thing that causes closet chaos is that which soothes our soul and makes us feel in control. Whether it's the Sale Sniper regulating choice with discounts or Tired & Emotional instilling calm with the familiarity of the past, it all boils down to the hang-ups driving the habits that shape your sartorial well-being. But is this *really* making your closet happy? Something tells me you wouldn't be reading this book if it were.

Recent studies carried out by University of Bath psychologists Paul Salkovskis and Sinead Lambe on the subject of hoarding delve deeper into the emotional pay-off theory – right back to those formative childhood years. Their study reveals that subjects used stockpiling as a coping mechanism to deal with various traumas from deprivation and restriction (austerity, things being taken away as a punishment) to family abandonment. In such cases, material things either became linked with the brain's reward centre or assumed an element of predictability in an otherwise unpredictable world.

We do our level best as humans to avoid the pain of loss, which would explain why we cling to the past even when it doesn't cater to our present needs. This underlying need to control our environment is a direct response to life's ambiguity. In order to get more comfortable with the act of decluttering, we've got to find our centre in the maelstrom and get accustomed to the notion of loss (however chaotic) in order that we may find more harmony. Sounds like hippie hokum? Why don't you find out for yourself?

Find your closet type on the Hang-ups, Habits and Happiness Chart opposite and examine the pay-off in relation to your hang-ups. Then figure out your wardrobe security blanket by looking back into your childhood to identify any patterns in your family life that could have provoked inclinations such as:

- The need to be noticed
- The need to hide things
- The need to stockpile.

Often, our fear-based habits have their roots in an underlying sentiment that no longer serves us, such as:

- I always felt dowdy as a child.
- There was never enough in our family.
- I never felt like I was enough.

HANG-UPS, HABITS & HAPPINESS

CORE TYPE	HANG-UPS (cue)	HABITS (method)	HAPPINESS (pay-off)
Impulse Buyer	Need to feel unique Impatience Insecurity	Trophy hunting Instant gratification Overspending	Newness feeds her desire to be noticed.
Secret Shopper	Secretive Lives in denial Values volume	Stashing Minimises spending Hoarding	Secrecy allows her to offset the judgement of others.
Doomsday Prepper	'Lack' mentality Insecure Reactive/fearful	Stockpiling Confuses need and want Overshops	Volume makes her feel prepared.
Tired & Emotional	Resistant to change Nostalgic Lives in the past	Hoarding Can't make decisions Comfort zoning	The past provides a safe space from the instability of the future.
Black Widow	Craves familiarity Fear of the new	Option paralysis Style default	Her style rut is easier than managing the constant onslaught of new trends.

CORE TYPE	HANG-UPS (cue)	HABITS (method)	HAPPINESS (pay-off)
Split Personality	Indecisive Compartmentalises Future-driven	Option paralysis Can't close doors No sense of self	Not having to choose means not having to give up something she might need.
Martyr Mom	Martyr syndrome Nostalgic Insecure	No sense of self Fear of the future Option paralysis	Dressing others is a way to avoid the insecurity of figuring out how to dress herself.
Sale Sniper	Need to feel unique Competitive Bargain-obsessive	Trophy hunting Bragging rights Quantity over quality	Bargains make her feel in control of her decisions in a world of choice.
Perfect 9	Perfectionist	Great overall habits but prone to overlooking her evolving self.	Potential complacency can cause a style rut.

Next, dust off that diary and write out the childhood scenario you feel best relates to your own wardrobe security blanket, similar to what you did in Chapter 2. Here, let me take the lead:

> I am the youngest in a big family. Having always been shy, I've found it difficult to be heard among the big personalities around me. As I grew up, I found my voice visually through clothes. I overcompensated for years of silence with bold fashion statements and gradually came out of my shell. Despite this, I never really learned to deal with my insecurities. Instead, I fed my fragile ego and desire to be accepted with my need to be seen.

Now, prepare a competing response that resonates with who you are *today*. I'll go first:

> Even though I am a grown woman, sometimes I feel like a child – especially at those times when I feel small and not heard. These moments are infrequent but when they do present themselves, I have a habit of falling into old routines. From now on, when I feel insecure or out of my depth, when I don't feel enough compared to others, I'm going to remind myself of how far I've come from that shy little girl, rather than feeding my ego (and my closet) with more clothes. Shining some light on the dark recesses of the past can go a long way to illuminating the present. As for the future? There's a happiness hack for that …

HAPPINESS HACK

Feeling the fear? Try one of these bite-sized closet cures.

Find fault in the default: What is it that makes you feel safe? Wearing black, notice-me labels? Covering your figure in baggy sweaters? Single out your security blanket and be mindful of its presence each time you feel swayed by its cosy charm. Ask yourself another question: how do you feel without it? Exposed? Incomplete? Sit with that feeling; allow yourself to feel uncomfortable. Feel its ambiguity. Then ask: what could you gain by letting go? What's the absolute worst thing that could happen? No one is going to frogmarch you into the town square and administer fifty lashes on account of not wearing this season's Chanel. Equally, the four horsemen of the apocalypse won't smite you for black-sacking that trailer-park trucker cap. Fire and brimstone is an Armageddon-only affair; besides, the sulphur smell is a nightmare to get out in the wash.

Good for: Black Widow

Get on board: Too scared to break from the past? There's an app for that. Pinterest.com, the social network scrapbooking site, allows 'pinners' (that's you and me) to create themed boards from online images. Use this as an opportunity to curate styles you'd like to try but never had the neck to buy. See what themes present themselves, then edit your board by deleting any items that don't fit in with the overall mood. Give yourself time to filter, feel and figure out what makes you tick – the real you who given half a chance and half the choice would actually have these pieces hanging in your wardrobe. Commit to buying and trialling a few pieces from the list that are outside your comfort zone and ask yourself how they feel. As your awareness is raised, the basal ganglia will begin to register this newness as an existing connection. Better still, the option to hide the board from public view also means your edit won't be seen by Nosy Noreen down the road. Nice one.

Good for: Tired & Emotional, Martyr Mom

Minimise choice: Shopping centres bamboozle me. Crowds of people, screaming children and interminable changing room queues cause total brain fog and before you can say 'dazed and confused', I'm sitting in Starbucks mainlining a grande Americano (with foam) while foaming at the mouth. This is not a good look. To preserve my vanity and make shopping excursions easier, I commit to mono-tasking – shopping for the one item that I need; no more, no less. By focusing on only one thing, I give my decision muscles a long lunch break and, as a result, always manage to find what I need rather than floating aimlessly with a half-baked idea of what I might want.

Good for: Impulse Buyer, Split Personality

Reframe the present: Remember your closet mantra from Chapter 1? Well, recite those three words like a magic spell. Programme it into your brain so that you believe you already have a 'harmonious, planned and co-ordinated' wardrobe (even if it does look like a tween slumber party). Use it as a yardstick every time you see something that catches your eye. Do those Rainbow Brite suspenders reflect your closet mantra, Ms Premium,

Cherished, Necessary? Nah, didn't think so. Now lay them on the floor and put your hands where I can see them ...

Good for: All closet types

Futureproof the now: Anxiety is a fear-based response to a future possibility. And as horoscope-reading, Dow Index-following, weather-predicting folk, we're partial to a bit of risk management. Nothing wrong with that. When caution turns into cold sweats over parting with a bag of mildewed sweatpants, then we've got trouble. The key to managing your state is futureproofing the now. Every time you start to feel your footing slide at the very mention of change, it's time to take a deep belly breath and get back to the present. So you need to throw a few things out? Focus on small bags, not the big picture. Get to grips with *why* you are decluttering and remind yourself of its life-affirming benefits: space, flow, calm. The minute your ego asks you what you'll do in the unlikely event of renewing your jaded gym membership, tell it to jog on.

Good for: All closet types

Desperate is as desperate does: Ever have a moment of next-level desperation? You know, a night at the local where after a recent break-up and seven vodka tonics, you find yourself Dysoning the face off that bloke who told you he was David Hasselhoff's cousin? 'But who else will love me?' you cry to your appalled friends. There, there. This lapse in clear thinking is less personal and more a primal response to scarcity. After all, things look more appealing when they're thin on the ground. Apply this analogy to your shopping habits and promise to *never* be that girl. *Please.*

Good for: Impulse Buyer, Secret Shopper, Split Personality, Sale Sniper

(Dis)own it: 'Throw them *out*? Those ass-less chaps are priceless!' Sounds familiar-ish? Ownership is a devil for creating emotional attachment, which, in turn, makes us overestimate the true value of our possessions. When wardrobe overwhelm comes a-knocking, follow everyone's favourite *Frozen* character and let it go. Cut the cord; bust a Buddha move and move on, chicken. A happy closet is one that feels good *now*. So unless you're auditioning for a Village People tribute act, detach with love.

Good for: All closet types

Question your motives: Every time you resist the need to declutter and replenish, it's time to call shenanigans on your unconscious mind. As Chapter 2 proved, behind every 'good' reason, there's an even better excuse. Question its made-up malarkey, dig for a deeper agenda and, basically, don't fall for the sob story. Feel the fear, be a dear and pay for its taxi home.

Good for: All closet types

Now that those mindfulness morsels have taken the edge off, it's time to really test those decision-making guns and give them a proper workout. Let's see if you can put the 'less is more' theory into action with a more challenging exercise. Here's a hint:

- What if you were fined each time you added something new to your wardrobe?

- What if you were charged excess baggage each time you carried your security blanket?
- Would you:
  a) carry less?
  b) carry on regardless?

Let's find out, shall we?

THE RYANAIR THEORY

'I get ideas about what's essential when packing my suitcase.'

DIANE VON FURSTENBERG

I remember it well. My friends and I were checking in at Dublin Airport en route to a sun-soaked Spanish holiday. According to Accuweather, it was due to be 'scorchio' which is meteorological speak for hotter than a sub-Saharan elephant's toe-cleft. We planned on wearing very little and getting very tan. So you could imagine their slackjaw scowl when my suitcase weighed in at a hefty 25 kilos. Unfazed, I released a jewellery-filled tote from deep inside its Samsonite jaws, deposited it into my carry-on and waited for the big reveal – 20 kilos on the button. Damn, I'm good. *Or so I thought.*

Why, I was asked, was I bringing a separate stash of beads, baubles and bangles, let alone all those clothes, to go from beach to bar? Was I preparing to moonlight at a Mr T Convention? Although the B.A. Baracus excuse could have proved a clever ruse, the truth of the matter was I was afraid of missing out on any and all potential opportunities for looking the part. Were a tycoon to invite us to an impromptu party at his mansion, I needed to know that my bases would be covered by more than just a sundress and flip-flops. It was my tenuous take on preparing to meet my fate. But had we all been flying Ryanair, this story might have begun and ended a lot differently.

If Ryanair has taught us anything, it's that excess has a price. Applying the low-cost airline theory of incontrovertible need to our definition of 'essential' transforms it into more absolutist terms. We humans do everything in our power to keep the maximum number of options open. In order to refine and define your style, you've got to learn to make calculated decisions and close doors.

The problem is that when faced with the issue of culling, emotion floods the brain, intercepting the channels of logic. We refuse to part with certain items even if they have passed their sell-by-date. Like kicking any habit or toxic pattern, if it's not adding value to your current lifestyle, then it should be swapped out for something with more purpose. Moreover, as we evolve as people, our clothing choices should too. Size, lifestyle, geography, career – these are all things that determine the shifts in our wardrobe needs. Hence why we need to keep abreast of our closets and not treat them as mere storage space.

Unless you're prepared to hire Michael O'Leary to pop out of your wardrobe and tell you to f*ck off every time you attempt to haggle for more hanger space, putting a premium on what you wear versus what you have can go a long way to increasing your happiness quota. The Ryanair rule is useful as a bridge exercise if culling seems all too big. It will help even the most hardened hoarder use their feelings to understand how excess is holding them back. Now, let's start unpacking ...

THE 10 KILO CHALLENGE

Having trouble separating need from want? It's time for some tough love – Michael O'Leary style. Your mission, should you choose to accept it, is:

- To create a capsule of interchangeable outfits for the next 14 days
- To pack it all in a 10 kilo bag, not exceeding the maximum dimensions of 55 cm x 40 cm x 20 cm.

The case is open. Your mouth is open. Just how in the name of blazes are you supposed to fit all of *that* into a tchotchke Ziploc bag, I hear you ask. Trust me, it *can* be done. The trick is to focus on the absolute essentials in order to bypass that territorial instinct discussed in Chapter 3. You know the old adage: give a woman a bag and she'll fill it for a day. Teach a woman to pack and she'll fill every damn bag she owns (or something of that ilk). Let's aim to flip that stereotype on its head. So where do you start? Simple.

- First, decide on a colour scheme – ideally two or three of the most common hues from your wardrobe.

- Using the guidelines below, adjust the contents according to your ratio of work, rest and play. It should look something like this:

2 bottoms	1 jacket
1 dressy bottoms	2 bags – 1 day, 1 night
1 jeans	1 sweater
2 tops	1 dress
1 dressy top	1 evening shoe
1 T-shirt	2 day shoes
1 coat	

- Ta da! This is your working wardrobe for the next fortnight.

- Keeping a record of the process in your diary, note how this makes you feel and how your emotions (nervous, anxious, empty, relieved) evolve throughout the weeks.

- Pay special attention to any items you thought you would miss:

  - Did you survive without those four extra pairs of jeans?

- ◆ How does the new sense of space feel: freeing, bare, stark?
- At the end of the two weeks, replenish and return the excess baggage to your closet.
- Continue to track your feelings in your journal for another week and record how you now feel about having more instead of less:
  - ◆ Is decision-making easier or more difficult?
  - ◆ Did you find an opportunity for creativity in being limited by choice or was it just a drag?
  - ◆ Did you quit? If so, why? Was the difficulty more to do with not having a solid foundation of basics, or having too many trends?
- Take time to scan through all your clothing:
  - ◆ Do you still feel the same way about everything?
  - ◆ Are there any pieces that don't seem as necessary any more?
- If you are ready, enlist that frank friend with no filter to make a cull.
- Let go and exhale.

So how did it go? Are you feeling the levity of a well-needed detox or can I expect a bounty on my head? I'm genuinely hoping it's the former. From my own experience with this exercise (yes, I've done it) and from those of my clients, the most common reactions are as follows:

Before:

- Are you high?
- Are you kidding me?
- I'm calling 999!
- What if I need (insert random accessory of no importance)?
- But I have a (insert random event of no importance) to go to this week.

After:

- I must be crazy. I can't believe I did that.
- It was difficult but definitely worth it.
- Now I get it.
- I really don't need all of this, do I?
- I think I'm ready for another closet clear-out.

As with any withdrawal regime, the initial restriction period can be a bit of a doozy but it invariably leads to a greater sense of clarity, energy and flow. Once you start reintroducing clothes back into your closet, you'll only want to wear those things that lend themselves to your sartorial well-being. Cluttering your closet with fads and trends will only make you feel sluggish again. So why go there? The challenge is in striking the balance between the staples that sustain wardrobe health with those sweet but short-lived fashion cravings. So, my lovelies, what's it going to be?

CHAPTER FIVE

TRENDS AND BASICS — LESS IS MORE IN ACTION

FINDING THE BALANCE

'Fashion kills the thing it loves.'

ANONYMOUS

The trend is a fickle mistress. One minute she's showering you with compliments; the next, she's throwing you major shade. It can be hard to keep up, which is precisely what makes her so alluring. Why else would she have so many suitors?

Ever mercurial, the trend has a unique ability to get into your head and make you do silly things like part with your hard-earned cash or obsess endlessly over an imagined future together. Taming her requires confidence and devil-may-care indifference. You don't want her to think you've tried *too hard*; that's when she'll turn the tables and skip town. Before you know it, you'll be left with nothing but a pile of barely worn clothes and the remote hope that she might circle back in a few years' time.

Basics, on the other hand, are unquestionably reliable. Unlike their capricious counterparts, they don't operate under self-appointed rules and exclusions. What you see is what you get. That said, they don't generate much heat. A bit like the missionary position, they do the job nicely – but in the world of fashion, nice guys finish last. Sometimes they don't finish at all.

The truth is, trends and basics have a symbiotic relationship. One adds flavour; the other adds substance. Need to amp up a plain shift dress? A brocade jacket ought to do the trick. While you're at it, dial down that leather skirt with a fitted polo neck and ankle boots.

Opposites do attract but, like any relationship, if compromise is lacking, then someone's going to be sleeping on the sofa. The key to a happy closet is all about balance. At best, trends should occupy no more than 30% of your wardrobe. Did someone say 'Boring'? I thought so. That's precisely my point.

Trends *feed* on boredom and our insatiable lust for the new. The more we're given, the more we want. It doesn't help that technology has completely rewired our expectations. Trends have been split like fashion atoms into micro-trends and fed to consumers weekly, daily, hourly. We don't just expect it; we demand it. So when this knee jerk response is not met, we get distracted and start sniffing around things that have no business in our closet, on our bodies or in our lives.

We've all been there but repeat offenders get little sympathy. There's a fine line between fashion victor and its less salubrious sidekick – victim. No one wants to be the saddo stuck with enough patchwork denim to warrant a B*Witched comeback (please, no).

But that's what happens when we get seduced by the exotic scent of newness. We give away too much and get very little in return. The trick is in playing it cool. A cheeky wink is often more impactful than a couch-jumping protestation of love. It suggests you've got something up your sleeve, which is far less embarrassing than wearing your heart on the outside of said sleeve. Far too revealing.

A bit of advice: treat trends as lovers, never as committed partners. They behave best when allowed a degree of distance, hinting at a look (a scintilla of sporty or pinch of preppy) as opposed to shouting about it. Trust me: you don't want the shouty ones. They'll only make a scene. What you want is a discrete sidekick – one that keeps coming back season after season. To do this, you'll need a vetting process to ensure you've identified the right type of trend that'll add value to your closet.

After all, not all trends are created equal. Some are exciting – like first-date butterflies; others are comforting – like ice-cream and *Golden Girls* reruns; and the rest are simply tiresome – like the drunk girl who doesn't know when to leave the party. Choose wisely; wear judiciously. Need a few pointers? Check out the trend roll call below.

HOW TO IDENTIFY A TREND

A trend is more than an indication of what's 'hot' right now. Those that stand the test of time tend to reflect a prevailing mood or attitude – the zeitgeist if you will. Trend forecasters (yes, they exist) act as Mystic Meg types for retailers and fashion houses, predicting what they believe will sell based on social, cultural and economic shifts – oh, and the weather too. Yep, that's right. If the *Farmers' Almanac* predicts a clanger of a winter, expect the Michelin Man to become fashion's unlikely muse. Think about it: did we ever hear of Festival Chic before people started frolicking to music in muddy fields? Would Boho still be flashing the peace sign without the '60s Summer of Love? And where would Hipsters be without Baby Boomer parents and pre-millennial nostalgia? Like 'em or loathe 'em, some trends have serious staying power, which makes them worthy of a heads-up. The trend roll call below isn't exhaustive as such. Consider it more of a Greatest Hits compilation – the oldies but goodies that keep the dance floor filled and the punters happy. You'll probably find you already have one or two of these chart-toppers already in your closet and maybe two more B-side singles you're attached to. If, however, you find yourself shaking your hips to each one, begging the DJ to play your jam, then we've got work to do. In the meantime, go find your groove, kiddo.

Goth Glam

Goth is glam alright but she's also a wee bit scary. Her deliciously dangerous wardrobe knows no boundaries and, to be frank, she doesn't give a sh*t: leather dresses at breakfast meetings, fetish boots on first dates, meeting the parents in PVC hotpants. Feared and adored in equal measure, she's the vixen you'd love to be, if only you had the balls.

Friends with: Grunge, Ladylike
Alter ego: Romantic

Boho

Winsome, sunkissed and carefree, Boho spends her time drinking craft beer and smoking herb ciggies at her boyfriend's gastro pub. She loves fringing, peasant tops, floaty kaftans and anything that may have been made in an ashram (authenticity is so 'now'). She has a job (we think) but her animal spirit guide told her to follow her bliss, so she's handed in her notice and is heading to Coachella – with the universe's blessing, of course.

Friends with: Romantic
Alter ego: Sports Luxe

Normcore

Normcore doesn't like to stand out. She hates the insane pressure of trophy dressing and so treads the path of least resistance in pool sliders and gym socks. Ironically, the ultra-conformist ease of Normcore has become a style statement in itself. She didn't plan on her dad sneakers and mom jeans creating a trendsetting love child but accidents do happen. She just hopes she's forgettable enough not to be confused with Hipster. Bland is the new black – who knew?

Friends with: Scandi Cool, Androgyne, Sports Luxe
Alter ego: High Maintenance

Sports Luxe

Sports Luxe is a model athlete. To clarify, she doesn't actually work out, but surely that's not the point? Styling tennis dresses and baseball jackets with the right amount of stretch panelling and peek-a-boo mesh is not easily achieved, which is why she balks at the charlatans who try to follow her lead. This is how wedge trainers became a thing, people. And we all know how that ended …

Friends with: Scandi Cool, Androgyne, Normcore
Alter ego: Boho

Grunge

Laissez-faire is the Grunge calling card. She may not live in Seattle, hang out in poetry cafés or rage against any machine, but this suburban office manager likes her share of counter-culture clothing. Although not prepared to go the whole Nirvana, she shows her fashionable disdain with a tartan skirt and artfully ripped sweater here, ripped tights and a babydoll dress there (very 'Kinderwhore') – but not to work, of course. Her ass would be totally fired.

Friends with: Goth Glam
Alter ego: Preppy

Androgyne

Gender holds no dominion over Androgyne. Not content to conform to stereotypes, she prefers subverting expectations with bolshie style choices: sharp tailoring, flat shoes (brogues do nicely) and a look of insouciant ease give 'Andy' the edge over her trend rivals. They may call her 'Manrepeller' but she doesn't care. She's not the one hobbling for a taxi every Friday night in 6-inch heels. Suckers.

> **Friends with: Scandi Cool, Normcore, Sports Luxe**
>
> **Alter ego: Ladylike**

Scandi Cool

Scandi Cool doesn't do sexy or super-stylish, yet her unstudied deference to utility makes her a scion for the intellectually disposed. Clean lines and geometric shapes feed into her abiding mantra of proportion. She understands that the right angle divided by the wrong length can equal an unstructured mess, which is why she's mastered the high fashion hypotenuse. Just don't expect her to tell *you* the formula.

> **Friends with: Androgyne, Normcore, Sports Luxe**
>
> **Alter ego: La Parisienne**

La Parisienne

La Parisienne *is* nonchalance. She knows it can't be taught (*c'est une 'attitude'*) but she also doesn't do guilt. If someone wants to copy her bare-faced chic and perfectly undone hair, why not? Whether they can create a Charlotte Gainsbourg homage with a vintage Chanel jacket and motocross skinnies is their headache. She does not concern herself with such trivialities. She's got a nap to take.

Friends with: Romantic, Boho

Alter ego: Scandi Cool

Romantic

Romantic is in love – in love with the idea of being in love. There's no better feeling than walking on candy-floss clouds covered in sparkles and tulle. Fantasy fuels her frothy collection of prom dresses, tiaras and kitten heels, which she wears whatever the weather – literally. So, there's an epic storm blowing; so, her toes are a bit frostbitten. Her mother always told her beauty was pain. Besides, Prince Charming will be along any minute now – *any minute …*

Friends with: La Parisienne, Boho

Alter ego: Goth Glam

Preppy

Preppy adores being preppy. It's her thing, so much so she named her three springer spaniels Cashmere, Khaki and Connecticut. Cute, no? She was tempted to buy them matching monogrammed cable-knit sweaters but she thought better of it. She gets enough heat for wearing topsiders and a popped collar, not to mention her unending fascination with the cast of *Made in Chelsea*. Oh, to be 'funemployed' …

Friends with: Ladylike

Alter ego: Grunge

Ladylike

Ladylike is part sphinx, part minx. Beneath that prim and proper exterior lies a feisty femme fatale. Of course, this delicious contradiction is key to her charm: tweed and pussy-bow blouses, corsets and silk stockings. If Ladylike had her way, she'd mandate that all 'leisurewear' be blowtorched in effigy. She's got standards to uphold.

Friends with: Preppy, Goth Glam (opposites attract)

Alter ego: Androgyne

Hipster

Hipster refuses to do mainstream but she's not averse to being noticed for it. Borrowing heavily from her granny's closet and '90s pop culture references (*Saved by the Bell*, anyone?), Hipster's look is a non-partisan political statement: self-reflexive enough to spoon-bend the word 'irony' but not so offensive as to completely alienate her fans. She didn't buy all those Instagram followers for nothing, you know.

Friends with: Other Hipsters; she doesn't do cross-tribe

Alter ego: Riviera

High Maintenance

High Maintenance is just that. She likes to wear her intent so that it is never mistaken. Ever. Monogrammed Birkin bag, next season's 'It' dress, RSI-inducing jewellery – if that doesn't give it away, she's going to start wielding a diamond-encrusted trophy in public and crying 'Get off my vineyard!' Hey, it worked on *Knot's Landing.*

> **Friends with: Riviera**
> **Alter ego: Normcore**

Riviera

La Dolce Vita is where it's at for Riviera – preferably on a yacht-strewn jetty raising a Campari glass alongside George Clooney – OK, *and* Amal. Her go-to garb? Capacious kimonos, white Capri pants, gold wedges, big bangles and even bigger sunglasses. She's been known to sport a turban for her boardwalk *passeggiata* but gave up the ghost when a freak gale wind blew it into the ocean. I guess that's what you deal with you live in Ireland.

> **Friends with: High Maintenance**
> **Alter ego: Hipster**

HOW TO INCORPORATE A TREND

So far we know that trends can be somewhat precocious, a bit precious and very unpredictable. We also know they can be a total hoot. But a happy closet needn't resemble a full-on house party in order to bring a smile to your face. The trick is to apply the 'less is more' theory to trends, limiting your closet to:

- 1–2 trends that best reflect your personality
- 1 trend that mirrors your alter ego.

Quick Psychology 101: the alter ego is the opposite of your true self. The poor sod gets a bad rap in popular culture, often portrayed as the dark side of our personality (see: Jekyll v. Hyde). In sartorial terms, things are a bit less binary. The alter ego can provide some helpful clues as to the unseen side of us that should get out to play more often. Cicero, first-century Roman philosopher, refers to the alter ego more kindly as 'a trusted friend'. This is the dude who's credited with inspiring the Renaissance, so my money's on him.

For instance, I'm Scandi Cool with a little bit of Ladylike. Strict silhouettes keep me on the straight and narrow but throw me a curve and some wiggle and watch me giggle. I have a client, on the other hand, who is strictly Normcore but whose happiest Closet Quiz purchase (see Chapter 1) is a pair of pink sparkly high heels. These Romantic beauties are perfect because the sprinkling of love dust helps give diversity to her collection of simple separates. Win win.

My sister, a corporate director, is the Boss Lady of Ladylike but, as we discovered earlier in the tale of the white jeans, she's got Riviera in her blood. Her one and only kaftan makes an appearance each spring in anticipation of the mercury rising as does her 'silly with excitement' face. Note: she just has one – not the entire Versace back catalogue (although I'm sure she wouldn't balk at that). Her kaftan's yearly appearance is enough to indulge her Riviera wish fulfilment but not so much that she believes she's Donatella's lesser-known twin – although when she starts referring to the rest of our family as *ragazzi*, I sometimes wonder.

If you happen to be a Split Personality, you might still standing there scratching your head. This is the perfect illustration of how trends trip you up if not managed carefully. By rights, trends should operate as an accent – a hint to the provenance of a look. The key is to make a trend look effortless, not to try hard. And the easiest way to achieve that is by integrating a trend with what you already own rather than compartmentalising it. Think interdependence not independence.

If you're a Goth Glam at heart, a Romantic lace dress will switch the mood of a tough leather jacket. Bit of a Boho? Add those fringed booties to a basic black dress for after-hours drama. If you're channelling the '70s, do it with a pinch of nostalgia and a healthy dose of presence. No one wants to be mistaken for an extra in the remake of *Staying Alive*.

Whatever you do, *don't* be trapped into thinking you need to buy a top-to-toe look around a specific item just because you saw it styled that way in a magazine. Glossy editorials are meant to spark the fires of fantasy, which, although deliciously indulgent, are also meant to sell product.

If in doubt, imagine swapping clothes with the model in that de luxe double-page spread and walking down your local high street/country lane/city block (delete as appropriate). Depending on your preferred reading material, this could be a conceptual cyber-warrior-priestess editorial or a mid-west prairie girl 'get the look' segment. How would it fly?

Then imagine taking one stand-out element from that look and adding it to a basic jeans and T-shirt combo. How does it feel now? More like you, I'd imagine. Toning it down doesn't mean extinguishing your natural light. Sometimes it's just a question of reducing the glare. That's basically how you incorporate a trend. Kind of basic, really? In case you didn't catch my drift, I've taken the liberty of fashioning a basics cheatsheet below. Just a basic one …

BASICS CHEATSHEET

I'm in no position to prescribe a remedy for closet happiness if your daily routine is sitting at home with a cuppa and the paper with not much else but central heating and a smile. What I will say is that sometimes the small things make life that bit easier. We all need to leave the house, go to work, greet our neighbours or attend an event that involves swapping our personal preferences for some (over)due diligence. Consider this your larder list − fill those wardrobe shelves and no one goes hungry.

Leave it to chance and you'll be shafted with a carrot and can of sweetened condensed milk when the in-laws pop round.

A Few Ground Rules

- Buy the best quality/cut you can afford.
- Stick to a neutral palette: white, cream, navy, black, tan, brown, khaki.
- Use trends and accessories to add flavour and colour.
- Choose pieces from the suggestions below that suit your shape, lifestyle and location (no point ticking high heels on the list if you live in the Alaskan tundra).

T-shirts – crew-neck or V-neck

Tank tops or camisoles

Long-sleeve tops – crew-neck or V-neck

Button-down shirt or blouse – in cotton or silk

Pencil skirt or full skirt

Ballet flats, loafers or brogues

Court shoes

Tailored blazer

Denim jacket

Denim shirt

Single- or double-breasted wool jacket or coat

Wax jacket or parka

Knee or ankle boot

V-neck or crew-neck sweater – in fine wool or cashmere

Indigo slim-cut or bootcut jeans

Slim-cut trousers

Structured bag

LBD

Clutch

Basic belt

Leather-strap watch

Sunglasses

Casual canvas shoe (Converse, tennis shoe, espadrille)

SIGNATURE STYLE

Picture this. You're at your local pub having a few after-work swifties and in walks Ellen de Generes. GOBSMACKED. While trying to act cool and most definitely not succeeding, you lean over to your friends and stage whisper, 'Sweet buttering baby Jesus! That's ELLEN DE GENERES!!!' They stare blankly. A cocked eyebrow here; a quizzical look there. 'Who?' one of them asks. You can't believe this. They're still on their first pint! You've got about five seconds in which to describe Ellen from head to toe before she turns around and spots you waving your arms like Dave the Rave. Your time starts now. Go!

5–4–3–2–1–STOP!

So, what was she wearing? I bet you found it easy to describe her: jeans, shirt and trainers; suit and T-shirt; waistcoat; brogues – variations on a theme. Get a few friends to do the same (obviously not the ones in the above scenario – they're clearly all pissed) and see how your answers compare. All fairly similar, am I right?

Think about it: have you ever seen Ellen in ruffles, a boob tube, strappy sandals? Nope, nope, nope. This woman's got a To Don't List, I'm sure of it. That's the beauty of someone with identifiable style – by limiting choice, they, in turn, create their own trademark or what in fashion speak is affectionately termed a 'signature'. Consider it a mindfulness tool, a sartorial statement of intent anchored in the present, which limits options to suit one's *self*.

The paradox of sticking to a signature style is that although it appears abstemious, it is, in fact, incredibly freeing. Some of fashion's most laudable figures are those who have created self-styled uniforms: a network of pieces that free the mind to concentrate on other things rather than be cluttered with the words 'What shall I wear?' In this way, signature savants have turned the dreaded default into a personal trademark by adding their own individual stamp to something intrinsically simple. The result? Pure magic.

Need some inspiration? Take a look at the panel of power players (past and present) from the world of fashion and showbiz who've proved that simplicity is its own reward.

Who: Ellen de Generes, award-winning talk-show host and actress

What: Reflects her warm, easy-going presenting style through comfy yet classic separates with tomboy ease.

Wears:

- Suits and T-shirts
- Shirts and jeans
- Sneakers and brogues
- Sweaters and vests
- Waistcoats

Who: Jenna Lyons, CEO of J. Crew clothing

What: Combines masculine cuts with feminine accents for gutsy girl-on-the-go style. Also quoted as saying she only takes three minutes to get dressed.

Wears:

- White shirts
- Black-rimmed glasses
- Centre- or side-part ponytail
- Bright lippie
- Tailored jackets and trousers
- Stiletto heels
- Print or textured accent (fabric or scarf)

Who: Katharine Hepburn, actress and political activist

What: Unconventional mould-breaker who put androgynous dressing on the style map.

Wears:

- White shirts

- Slacks
- Loafers
- Shirt dresses
- Wide silhouettes
- Culottes

Who: Diane Keaton, actress, director, producer and screenwriter

What: *Annie Hall* alum known for wearing clean monochromatic lines with an offbeat edge and bohemian brio.

Wears:

- White shirts
- Black trousers
- Tuxedos
- Black-rimmed glasses
- Bowler hats and berets

Who: Grace Coddington, US *Vogue* creative director and revered stylist

What: Embraces a pared-back style sensibility so that her visionary photoshoots are the focus of attention.

Wears:

- Monochrome
- White-tab collars
- Black trousers
- Black coats

- Flatforms
- Shock of Titian-red hair

Who: Diane von Fürstenberg, fashion designer, philanthropist and former princess

What: Revolutionised fashion with the wrap dress, giving the working woman a de facto a.m.-to-p.m. uniform.

Wears:

- Desk-to-dinner dresses — wrap, shirt, beaded, day, evening, cocktail
- Roomy shapes
- Punchy prints
- Sexy heels
- Pre-Raphaelite long curly bob

Who: Carine Roitfeld, French *Vogue*'s former editor-in-chief

What: Chic nonconformist who put the term 'age-appropriate' back in its silly box — and rightly so!

Wears:

- Silk shirts
- Sexy pencil skirts
- Towering heels
- Shoulder-slung tailored coats
- Goggle-style sunglasses
- 'Oh-I've-been-naughty' bed head hair

Who: Kate Middleton, HRH the Duchess of Cambridge

What: Praised for her unwavering practicality, this royal is no princess when it comes to wearing the same thing twice. We approve.

Wears:

- Nude courts, kitten heels and wedges
- Midi-length and shift dresses
- Nude tights
- Classic-cut coats
- Side-parted shoulder-length hair

Who: Michelle Obama, First Lady of the USA

What: Mixes high-street labels with high-end designers for a more populist than presidential approach to dressing. Believes in business casual and the right to bare arms.

Wears:

- Shift dresses
- Cardigans
- Double-strand pearls
- Full skirts
- Kitten heels
- Detailed belts

CREATING YOUR SIGNATURE

If you haven't quite figured out what makes your look unique, then it's time to create your signature mantra. Like the closet mantra in Chapter 1, your signature creates an aspiration for your look – a future perfect tense. The aim is to get you working towards a wardrobe that is determined by you and your present needs. The great thing is that as you evolve and your personal circumstances change, you can simply repeat the process until those numinous words become concrete style signposts. Are you ready? Good. It's time for a game of word association.

The Three Fs

Your aim with this exercise is to select three words that best reflect the Three Fs of any closet: feeling, feature and fit. Ask yourself: does what's inside answer the following questions?

- Feeling: 'How do I feel?'
- Feature: 'How does it look?'
- Fit: 'What is the shape?'

For instance, my signature mantra is:
- Feeling: Elegant
- Feature: Minimal
- Fit: Clean

Whereas Ellen de Generes would most likely choose:
- Feeling: Laidback
- Feature: Preppy
- Fit: Tailored

Need some pointers? The chart on the next page illustrates three types of words that lend structure to your signature.

FEELING	FEATURE	FIT
'How do I feel?'	**'How does it look?'**	**'What is the shape?'**
sophisticated	textured	sleek
current	embellished	clean
free-spirited	minimal	soft
creative	lacy	sharp
unpredictable	stripy	crisp
light-hearted	sparkly	body-conscious
elegant	patterned	voluminous
laidback	shiny	tailored
coquettish	colourful	loose
eclectic	accessorised	fitted
adventurous	neutral	strict
ballsy	ethnic	relaxed
cosy	Gallic	classic
poised	bohemian	revealing
offbeat	luxurious	dramatic
nerdy	effortless	avant-garde
wild	urban	sporty
independent	preppy	ladylike
artsy	futuristic	loud
confident	punk	bold
breezy	rock	floaty
edgy	ornate	structured
romantic	retro	uniform
quirky	opulent	unstudied
comfortable	womanly	fluid
conservative	androgynous	functional

Avoid generic words like 'chic', 'stylish', 'fashionable' or 'individual'. These simply describe the end-game and are a bit clichéd. If you're fed up with your current style statement, think of something that's aspirational yet manageable and make that your goal.

Play around with combinations, try them on for size, see how they feel. Once you've mastered your mantra, repeat it out loud. How does it sound? It's easy to know what looks like 'you' but the oral resonance of saying it loud can be really impactful.

There's no point aiming for light-hearted, embellished and voluminous if you're serious, understated and refined at heart. Think back to the Ellen exercise: add in the words tomboyish, preppy and tailored to the list of what she's wearing and you'd surely hammer it home to your hammered friends. While you are planting the seeds of change in your subconscious, here are a few more grounded tips you can plant straight into your closet.

HAPPINESS HACKS

Follow the Pareto Principle: Otherwise known as the 80–20 rule, Pareto's Principle states that 80% of the effects come from 20% of the causes. Put simply, it's time to figure out which 20% of your wardrobe is resulting in 80% of your happiness. Need a hint? Look back to the 10 Kilo Challenge and you've got your answer.

Bulk up on basics: It bears repeating: basics are the staples of a happy closet. They keep you looking 'put-together' even when you're falling apart. Individually, they are simple; combined with more extravagant pieces, they come into their own. When in doubt, think of the humble tee: it has the ability to make both jeans and a formal skirt look incredibly cool. Big love for the little guy. The same goes for any of his unassuming friends such as crisp shirts, tuxedo jackets, pencil skirts and tailored trousers.

Upgrade with accessories: Don't underestimate the power of a well-placed necklace or better-than-sex bag to completely reinvent an outfit. What appear to be trinkets are, in fact, veritable amulets of change. Not only do they provide a low-commitment approach to tackling trends, their cost-per-wear ratio is unparalleled. And who doesn't love a gorgeous shoe?

Find your 'me' piece: 'That's so me', 'that's so her', 'that's so you!' You've said it, you've heard it, you've repeated it. Whether it's a silk shirt, a bouclé jacket or a beat-up pair of Levis – if it feels like you and others identify you with that piece, then make like Anna Wintour's tan sandals and wear it as the linchpin of your look.

Be intuitive: Intuition is the best arbiter of what works and what doesn't. Always heed her wise counsel. If a white shirt makes you feel more corporate than cool – don't wear it. Never one to say 'yes' to the dress? Why not say 'yes' to trousers instead? Debating too long over what you *should* wear is as detrimental as giving in to impulsive behaviour. The difference between intuition and an impulse? Intuition is calm and collected. She knows what she wants; no explanations needed. Impulses, on the other hand, run around like pups let off their leads – licking, jumping, barking.

Granted, they're fun to be around, but one of them will always pee on your leg and then shoot you those guilty brown eyes. Intuition would've seen that mess coming.

Limit trends: Put boundaries on these bad boys lest they multiply and eat into your closet space like furry little gremlins. Select one or two styles that work best with your basics and leave wiggle room for an alter-ego accent — one off-the-wall piece that adds fun and frisson. Done and done.

OK. We've covered a lot of ground. So, what do we know so far?

- Habits won't stick unless you know who you are.
- Limiting your options creates more ease and allows for smarter choices.
- Knowing what you won't wear is key to understanding your personal style.
- Trends work better as accents rather than a foundation.
- Balance is about prioritising needs before indulging in wants.

Sounds like a lot of pain and no gain? Quite the contrary. This is not a hair-shirted philosophy (they're far too scratchy). If anything, the 'less is more' theory is liberating when executed on *your* terms. Prescriptive fashion epithets like '10 Things Every Woman Should Own' have no place in a happy closet. Each hanging space is unique to its personal fears, joys, hopes and experiences. The real solution in creating lasting closet happiness is in mastering what habit mastermind James Clear calls 'identity-based habits' – those behaviours which reflect your true self. These are the buckos that will stick like a tongue to a cold pane of glass (not that I've ever licked a window, of course not).

Lists are merely curated lifestyle suggestions based on somebody else's notion of what constitutes 'need'. There's no point investing in a Chanel 2.55 bag if you much prefer that top-handle tote from the local car-boot sale. Why buy a 'classic' trenchcoat if you can't walk through the park without feeling like Freddie the Flasher? Find what gives you joy and wear it until your heart hurts. The key is in separating lust from love. We've all been there, done that and worn the rose-coloured specs – that all-too-familiar Britney moment when 'Oops!', you plum went and did it again. Will you ever get it right? Fear not. My shingle is out and the chaise-longue awaits. It's time for some long overdue relationship advice …

CHAPTER SIX

WHAT'S YOUR RELATIONSHIP LIKE?

THE HEART OF THE MATTER

'Love makes one so receptive to everything beautiful.'

CLARA SCHUMANN

We all have a relationship with our clothing. Some of us have a sustained bond built over time; others, a carnal rip-'em-off-in-the-changing-room lust; then there are those who practise rigorous ascetic detachment – sartorial celibacy, if you will. Suffice to say, the degree to which we connect with what's on the outside all boils down to what's happening on the inside. Like it or not, our clothing reflects more than our external appearance; it also conveys our thoughts, feelings and habits at a given moment in time. Slipping on a shirt and a skirt is more than just getting dressed; it's an act of intimacy. How you relate to this (offhand or hands-off, chance or intention) is a measure of conscious awareness.

Trippy? Perhaps, but let's be honest: we have an emotional connection with what we wear that is at once transformative and talismanic. Why else would Glenda the Good Witch have given Dorothy a pair of ruby slippers? Clicking those heels did more than get Miss Garland back to Kansas; they manifested magic – that sweet spot where memories are made.

Do you think having four back-up pairs bought on sale for €9.99 would have had the same effect on that yellow brick road to self-discovery? Not quite. They may have gotten her mid-west caboose out of Oz but they're hardly the stuff of storytelling – and most certainly not the heart's desire.

Only you can decide whether what's behind that wardrobe door is hindering or helping your happiness. Are you getting what you need from your wardrobe or, indeed, are you putting in the necessary graft? If you want to build a happy closet, you'll need to get honest in order to reap the rewards. You'll also need to be gutsy enough to let go if something isn't working.

Vulnerability is the cornerstone to real intimacy, so if you want more purpose than potential, you'd best learn how to separate the one-night stands, fashion flings and online swipes from the love that's worth saving. Is it time to make up or break up? Let's see, shall we?

REAL LOVE

My most prized possession is my father's Claddagh ring. It was given to me by my mother as a Christmas gift when I was 14. As he passed away when I was just 4 years old, it was more than just a gift – it was a treasure. For the next 24 years that ring took pride of place on my index finger, never to be removed – until it disappeared. The irony? I had left it on top of my jewellery box as it was feeling a bit loose. I didn't want to lose it. A few hours later, it was gone. *Thanks Universe.*

After two days of scouring the house, moving furniture, dissecting the vacuum bag and discovering a host of dislodged socks, I called on the big guns – divine intervention. I prayed to St Anthony – patron of lost things (no answer); I prayed to St Jude – chief bottle-washer of lost causes (still no answer). Since Anto and yer man Jude were on voicemail, I proceeded to hit up every other conceivable saint in the Catholic canon: St Lucia – guardian of fashion designers and blind people (surely I fall into the latter category); St Eligius – the grand Poobah of goldsmiths and jewellers. I even hit up St Severus, the big cheese for drapers, milliners, silk workers, weavers and wool manufacturers – just to cover my bases. Still no word.

Fast-forward nine months and a lot of crying later and a golden circle of heart-holding hands appeared like Bobby Ewing in the shower. Only unlike said reprised Dallas character, it was stuck in a pair of bejewelled sandals. More fitting, surely.

The moral of the story? If it were a knicknack or trinket, I wouldn't have missed it – or possibly even realised it was missing. The things we hold dearest give us the most joy (and heartache when we lose or damage them).

Chances are it wouldn't have even been on my finger. When you swap the mindset of disposability for something indispensable – that's when something truly profound happens. Closet happiness isn't an austerity measure. It's about measuring what's of value and wearing it until you wear it out. Sometimes it outwears the wearer. That's when you pass it down the line and keep the love alive.

HAPPINESS HACK

What do *you* value most? (Hint: check your answers to Question 12 in the Closet Quiz!) Grab your diary and jot down the feelings and memories that come up for you. Next, close your eyes and sit with these feelings. Allow them to settle into your brain and body. Replay the memories in your mind and notice how these feelings lift your mood. Repeat this exercise a few times until the feeling becomes automatic each time you think of it. Continue to use this as your GPS – the gold standard for how you feel about your clothes.

FASHION FLINGS & ONE-NIGHT STANDS

Everyone's got a dirty little secret hiding somewhere in their closet. Fact. We've all fallen prey to the quickie, the fashion fling, the one-night stand. If there's anything that provokes sartorial shame, embarrassment or the words 'What was I thinking?', it's the 'wham-bam-thank-you-ma'am' moment.

I'm not saying it's the heated act of lust that's at stake here. It's more to do with our judgement when we come face to face with the object of our desire. Are we thinking long-term? Do we consider quality? Never. Once those happy hormones hit the brain's pleasure centre, all bets (or rather, clothes) are off.

Much like 'beer goggles', certain clothes hit us with a cocktail of chemicals that tap into the brain's 'desire and reward' response. Adrenaline, dopamine and serotonin dupe us into taking risks and before you can slap a condom on your credit card, the brain's reflexive mental processing has kicked in and you find yourself building self-serving excuses around the object of your desire:

'I usually don't do this sort of thing.'

'Once can't hurt.'

'What the hell. You only live once!'

'This is so unlike me.'

Waking up to the realisation that you'll actually never wear a pair of €700 fur-lined Birkenstocks in rainy Dublin is when reality really starts to sink in – especially when you can't find the receipt. Here's a clue: if sheer mortification forbids you from donating it to a charity shop or a recycling bin lest it is somehow linked back to you, then you've definitely had the ride – or, at the very least, been taken for one.

The only way to foster a meaningful relationship with your wardrobe is by avoiding the quick fix – but that takes some conscious reprogramming, something we'll get to a little later. The magnetism of instant gratification is part of our ancestral hardwiring. No prizes were given to our cave kin for thinking before doing. Immediacy had its own reward – namely, staying alive.

Cultivating an awareness of how our present actions will affect the future (crush or commitment, fling or affinity) creates the necessary space to see what it is that adds tangible practical and emotional value to our lives. Taking a breather and gathering your thoughts is a lot easier when your proverbial knickers aren't already hanging around your ankles and, as we all know, the hangover of our less-than-perfect decisions lingers much longer than the dalliance itself. Much of the reason for our regret is a lack of planning. Speaking of which …

WEDDING FEVER

If there's one word that inspires fear, loathing and credit card debt in the hearts of women, it's 'wedding'. All it takes is an innocent 'Save the Date' invitation to make us lose our reason and do things we live to regret.

Regret may seem a strong word here but trust me, I've got the goods on this one. Cast your mind back to Question 12 a) in Chapter 1's Closet Quiz: 'What was your most regrettable purchase?' I'd guess it's probably something you wore once and never wore again. Am I right? Would I also be correct in imagining it might have been something for a wedding? Ha! I knew it! *Damn, I'm good.*

Fear not. We've all fallen foul of wedding fever at some point in our lives. Symptoms often include (but are not limited to): cold sweats; mounting anxiety; periodic lashing out over a one-off wonder that is generally bought in a rush, at great expense and under immense stress for an occasion you are obliged to attend. Often triggered by the need to impress and the assumption that you cannot wear the same outfit twice. Pain is acute and intense but can be quickly relieved by removal of offending garment and a burning ritual. If unsure of whether your regret twinges may, in fact, be nuptially induced, check if any of these signs ring a wedding bell.

Stages of Wedding Fever

- Roll eyes and exclaim, 'Great, another wedding. What am I going to wear?'
- Allow vitriol to subside and gradual panic to set in.
- Avoid checking your wardrobe for options. Where's the fun in that?
- Instead, ruminate endlessly about who's been invited, how many of the same guests were at the last wedding and whether this function requires an added dose of one-upmanship.
- Buy inordinately expensive hat and obscenely high heels.

Stare at combo as if they were new-fangled sex toys while figuring out how they work and potential health risks.

- Wait until last minute to buy dress.
- Spend an entire day running like Anneka Rice from pillar to post on the hunt for matching frock.
- Find 'treasure' five minutes before closing time.
- Convince yourself you have every intention of wearing canary yellow taffeta again.
- Attend wedding.
- Simmer in rage for four hours.
- Untag any and all incriminating social media posts.
- Remove outfit and put into back of wardrobe.

It's ironic that we wear the clothing equivalent of a one-night stand to weddings but our closets are full of them. What is truly flabbergasting is how willing we are to repeat the process – lest the first three times weren't traumatising enough. And it all comes down to one home truth: the need for external validation. If we weren't bothered by what Aunty Mary and our third cousin once removed on our mother's side thought, we'd make like Kate Middleton and wear the same dress twice. Now there's a woman who gets royal flak for essentially being a rebel – flouting public perception and setting her own standards. *Nice work missus.* So the next time you find yourself coming down with a case of wedding fever, consider these handy wedding outfit questions.

Instead of asking:

- Do I love it?
- Will I wear it again?
- Do I want to marry it? (*Kidding but not kidding*)

We ask:

- Will everyone else love it?
- Will someone else be wearing the same one?
- Can I pawn this off on Done Deal?

We need to start looking at clothing as potential partners as opposed to 'alright for the night'. Granted, it's nice to have a warm body in the bed but if you'd prefer not to be seen in public with said body, then we have a problem. Start by asking, 'Would I wear this again even if I had another option?' If the answer is 'yes', you've got a keeper. Otherwise, leave it on the hanger where it belongs.

THE RELATIONSHIP NCT

Every relationship needs an emotional NCT: a quick heart scan to see if those feelings that drove the initial bond are still there. Open your wardrobe doors. Examine each garment (clothing, shoes, accessories) and rate it on a relationship scale of 1 to 10: 1 being one-night stand, 5 being casual dating and 10 being life-long lovers. Ask yourself the following questions before grading each piece:

1. How did we first meet?
2. Was it love at first sight or a slow burn?
3. How long have we been together?
4. Where and when do we normally go out? e.g. to work; only on weekends; to parties; every day and everywhere.
5. How do I feel when I am wearing it?
6. Has it ever let me down? If so, how?
7. Is there a similar item in my wardrobe that competes for my affections? If so, how does it compare and why?
8. What is it about this garment that makes it a keeper?
9. Why are we still together?
10. Do I see a future with it?

Whether it's a love-worn leather jacket or a cocktail dress that only emerges for swanky soirées, it should score at least a 7. Items that hover between 5 and 7 need a relationship talk. Put them on probation for another month and make an effort to start wearing them again. If a sartorial spark fails to reignite, be mature and break up. Alternatively, a trial separation can test the value of your relationship. Store away those items that only scored a 5 or 6 for a month. See if you miss them. If not, break up; don't make up. Anything under 5 needs to go – stat. All these items are doing is taking up valuable hanger space that could be occupied by more suitable partners or, indeed, left empty.

Emptiness. It scares us, doesn't it? Funnily enough, it's this very space – the pause, the ellipsis – that gives us the chance to breathe and to appreciate what's right in front of us. Why have 25 dresses on stand-by if you only have eyes for one? And if nothing special comes to mind, it's possibly because there's a packed rack of 'just in case' blocking the view.

BREAKING UP

Sometimes love makes us do stupid things, like continuing to shop at certain places that just don't deliver on their promises: all talk, no trousers. We can't help ourselves though, can we? Like flies to a pane of glass, we continue to bash our little heads against its shiny exterior in the hope that it might open. Where one window closes, though, there's always an open door and in this case, it says 'exit'. Put simply, when zips break, seams split and indecent exposure looms large, it's time to pen the proverbial 'Dear John' letter and bow out gracefully. No good can come of it otherwise – trust me.

Dear John,

It pains me to have to write this but some things just need to be said. You know we've always had such a special relationship. But lately, things have changed.

It all started with those flimsy hems. I was prepared to overlook having to Bondaweb that maxi-skirt, especially when I received so many compliments wearing it. You always knew how to make a girl feel pretty, didn't you? I even bought a second one in black, only to have you let me down in the same way again. A hem seemed a small indiscretion in the greater scheme of things. You were my haven, my sanctuary. When I was with you, time stood still and I got carried away by the sheer novelty of it all.

Nevertheless, I just wasn't prepared to let you go – not until the zip incident, that is. It literally happened behind my back and I was just too stupid to see it. How could you just embarrass me like that in the middle of the street? I'm just thankful I wasn't wearing a thong. I really don't know if I could ever truly trust you again.

So this is goodbye. Don't think you can tempt me with those new mohair sweaters that arrived this week. I got your email and I'm not falling for it. You'll just shed all over me. Really, there's only so much one person can take.

I'm through.

Yours (*was*),

Annmarie

HAPPINESS HACKS

Don't settle: The words 'it'll do' never did anything. Don't simply buy something because it is adequate. The more you make do, the more you'll be prepared to compromise. Hold out for the one; save for the one; be excited about the one. Whether it's the texture of a soft cotton T-shirt or the hand-stitching on a one-of-a-kind opera coat – you have to *want* to wear it, not *have* to wear it. Facial wipes are handy; a festival port-a-loo is adequate. Clothes should occupy neither category. Good enough is exactly what's got you here. Go for the big love, not a failed romance.

Good for: Tired & Emotional, Black Widow, Martyr Mom

Stop trying to make it work: This is a simple adage by which we should all shop. If it doesn't work now, it won't ever work later. So stop *trying* to make it work. When something is right – be it a relationship or a pair of jeans – it just fits. There's an ease about it. You don't need to create clauses and conditions to justify its presence. Phrases like 'I might get wear out of it yet' need to go. If you haven't been motivated to wear it yet (which is kind of the point in having bought it), then its presence is pointless.

Good for: All closet types

Differentiate between lust and love: Lust is a craving – an overwhelming urge that masters you. Love, to paraphrase St Peter, is the mastery of patience. If you're really busting a gut over wanting to buy something – wait. That lip-smacking 'come hither' hankering will soon subside. If it is replaced by a 'you complete me' kind of buzz, then slap my knee and call me an old softie. She's yours. Go buy her!

Good for: Impulse Buyer, Secret Shopper, Split Personality

Don't be swayed by the lookers: A word of warning: just because it's beautiful doesn't mean it's a keeper. Hanger appeal is just that. What drapes dramatically from curved wooden shoulders may fall flat on yours. I once dated a guy with bone structure that would make angels weep with joy but when he opened his mouth, time stood still, birds fell from the sky and I asked 'Why, God? Why?'. Take time to consider your options. Work outside your comfort zone. Often the pieces we overlook are those that look best.

Good for: All closet types

Don't accept sloppy seconds: Your sister gave you that top that doubles as a two-person tent? Guess what? She didn't want it either. Joke's on you. How can you expect to form a real relationship with your clothing if you don't do the choosing? This is not a Jane Austen novel. You don't need members of your family to furnish you with sartorial alms. You're a big girl now. Now start dressing like one.

Good for: Tired & Emotional, Martyr Mom

Leave the past in the past: That bag you purchased in college? You know, the beer-stained tote that wondrously carried lecture notes, tins of beans, toilet paper stolen from the arts block stalls and also doubled as a handy draught excluder? She's looking a bit tired. No, a lot tired. We know you've got history (and she's got major dirt on you) but it's time to consign your partner in crime to that big recycling bin in the sky. The aul bag needs a nap.

Good for: Tired & Emotional

Accept your part: The zip isn't closing on your favourite skirt. Typical – that always happens. And those heels you bought last week are too tight. No one *ever* does half-sizes. As for button gape on shirts – nightmare! You can never seem to find the right fit. That's why you hate shopping. I mean, why bother, it's such a hassle. Ladies: perception is nine-tenths the of the law. You will reach pay-dirt with a bit of effort but, in the words of Mike Robbins, 'nothing changes until you do'.

Good for: Tired & Emotional, Black Widow, Martyr Mom

It's not you; it's me. It's the cliché we love to hate but one that applies to any closet-related relationship. As we evolve, so do our needs. If you've no longer got any room in your life for whatever is taking up space, it needs to go. This assumes added gravitas when coupled with the phrase 'I used to wear that all the time' – which loosely translates as 'and I haven't put it next or near my body since 2001'. Frequently combined with a nostalgic head tilt and a well-intended sigh. You know the drill …

Good for: All closet types

DATING VS SHOPPING

Much of my single life has been spent doing things that aren't dating, despite wanting a partner. Doesn't make sense now, does it? It gets better. Each time I'd go on the odd date that turned out less than satisfactory, I'd swear off men and wonder why I was still single. Dating for me meant pain and we humans do whatever we can to avoid its mere suggestion.

When I did get the gumption to go back on the scene, I'd invariably be sidelined by a knock-back, no-show or one-date wonder, enough to dent my ego and convince myself that celibacy was, in fact, a viable option. Lo and behold, I'd wind up having my meal-for-one with a generous helping of self-serving bias.

It occurred to me that I wasn't giving this dating lark much of a go in order to make it work – *really work*. Granted, there were some hard acts to follow: the amateur rapper-turned-aquaponics enthusiast, the Shutterstock model ('man laughing with salad') and that taxi driver who offered me a 'free' lift home – but if I *really* wanted to find a full-time fella, I had to put in consistent and regular graft. You know where this is going.

Closet happiness is no different. If you want dressing to be more heartfelt than heartache, you've got to start by committing to the process. That means shopping with intent.

Sure, you might meet a few clangers along the way (keep those receipts!) but in time your resolve will strengthen and you'll start to see improved results. Practical application, whether shopping for love or for clothes, is the only reliable method. Granted, there are some who luck out, led by the gentle hand of serendipity to their soulmate – not dissimilar to those blessed with an ineffable knack of making anything from a bin-liner to a panty-liner look stylish. Suffice to say, such folk are few and far between. The rest of us operate by trial and error.

Finding your personal style groove is a lot like finding the right partner. Some of you will find the love of your life straight away, while others will come across stalkers, catfish and next-level stranger danger. The guarantee? There are no guarantees. Like most things in life, you get out what you put in. Allow your pursuit of closet happiness to be an ongoing process, not simply an end result. The more you apply yourself, the more you'll discover about yourself along the way. And no, I haven't been sniffing the incense again. I'm just giving you a kindly heads-up on how to commit to making this gig work – for you. So what are you waiting for? It's time to go shopping!

PLAN OF ACTION

'Fail to plan, plan to fail.'

HILLARY RODHAM CLINTON

Here's the deal. You've got to approach shopping like a woman on a mission. Intention is everything. There's no wiggle room for time-wasters, faffers or dilly dalliers. Window-shopping is only permissible if you are actually in the market for a new window; the same goes for browsing – leave it to Google. Now that you're clear on how and why to strengthen your relationship with your closet, it's time to create a plan of action to ensure you commit to your values while out in the field. After all, the perfect wardrobe doesn't just happen. You make it happen. Now, let's do this.

HAPPINESS HACK

BEFORE

Create space in your schedule: Make an appointment to shop. By crafting regular shopping time, it won't get to boiling point of need, which will, in turn, intercept the regret missile hurtling towards you at the rate of knots. Don't have much time on your hands? Smaller regular chunks do the same (if not more) than blocking off a full day. If you set time limits, you're more likely to stick to what you need.

Dress for the occasion: If you are to shop with any hallmark of intent, you'd best dress comfortably. Have you ever negotiated a changing room in a pair of tights, laced knee-high boots and a button-down dress layered over a polo neck sweater with a belted coat and some furry mittens? Ask yourself, 'How can I do this easily and effectively over a span of four hours without collapsing like a flopsy doll?' Opt instead for a comfy dress, slip-on shoes, drawstring trousers – anything that helps facilitate, not impede the process. Furthermore, if you need heels or special undies to try on a dress, bring them with you. If a recipe called for milk, would you make the dish without it?

Put some fuel in the tank: All of you after-work, lunch-break or on-the-fly shoppers: listen up. Make sure you have eaten before you start any sort of retail mission. There is a clear and documented link between willpower and our blood sugar levels, which will effectively clap out like an iPhone battery if not refuelled every couple of hours. The more tired our brain, the poorer our decisions and the higher our level of regret. Keep some snacks and a bottle of water in your handbag. When it comes to closet health, this is one of the few occasions where regular caffeine breaks are accepted, if not encouraged.

DURING

Control your environment: Give yourself an objective and stick to it. Shop environments can either repel or seduce, depending on the time of day, the number of rogue children and whether your parking fairy is sleeping on the job. Best advice? Go off-peak and get the heck out of Dodge before crowds begin to surge – usually around 11 a.m. and always before lunch. Ideally, go shopping alone but if you need a second option, bring that frank friend with no filter or one with no agenda. Buy him or her lunch and a few glasses of wine in exchange for their time and attention. There's nothing worse than someone hijacking your valuable shopping hour to feather his or her own nest.

Look to the label: Read the fine print. If a jacket is dry-clean only and you've got two kids under two and a full-time job, then it's got 'high maintenance' written all over it. A cool-wash alternative may be just what you need. There's no joy in wearing something for two minutes only to find an errant poo smear from your little dear and no way of cleaning it that doesn't involve a hefty charge and a week-long wait. Where's the fun in that?

Find the connection: There's nothing wrong with buying a 'well, blow me down and call me Dusty' piece that just deserves to be worn. Nothing at all. Where we run into a spot of bother is when it has zero relation to what's already in our closet. If there's no dialogue, then regardless of how gorgeous it is, it'll be hanging on its own like Nelly No Mates and you'll be obliged to buy it friends who speak its language. Repeat this process one too many times and your closet will be like the Tower of Babel. Rule of thumb: do not create a life around a love interest. Instead, make sure it fits in with your existing picture.

Keep focused: Distraction by design is a fitting catchphrase for the modern shopping landscape. Overwhelmed by choice, we prefer to make quick and familiar decisions rather than using up our precious attention supplies. That's why multi-tasking is so damn tempting. We can graze and surf in a fraction of the time and ultimately get more done, right? Wrong. Multi-tasking barely scratches the surface, relying on the shortcut of familiarity to get the job done. What's more, it is argued that the brain can only process an average of seven pieces of information at a time, give or take two, which would explain why we always forget something on our shopping lists. Want to shop with intent? Start mono-tasking: tackle one item at a time from a list of five items – no bigger.

Delay gratification: Neuroscience studies prove that when dopamine tickles the brain's pleasure receptors, it can take a full 30 minutes to recover. The only way to is to walk away. Use bargaining tools (much like we do with children) to dampen the desire. Tell yourself you can buy it tomorrow. Check in with how you feel. Play the scenario out in your head – will that diaphanous babydoll dress cut it at the parent–teacher meeting, walking the dog, at dinner with the board of directors, or are you simply convincing yourself it will? This will allow time for the brain to figure out whether this is a need or simply a want that can wait.

AFTER

Seeing is believing: Don't hide your haul. Much like credit cards, stashing creates a deferred reality between what we buy and what we admit to having bought. Taking stock of your closet collateral leads to a more revealing emotional inventory by confronting the underlying behaviour. Start by removing every item from its bag or box and hang it up. Then, address the sum of your closet's parts. Where you identify your style default, any doubles or simply dead weight, remove the offending items, bag them up and return – tout de suite, my sweet.

Try it on for size: We don't always try before we buy. Sometimes the thought of body-surfing a wave of people to the changing rooms for the sake of a top is a stretch too far. In instances such as these, do the honours at home – immediately. Try it on with a few different things. Photograph how it looks. Sit, stand, walk around; get comfortable; try with heels, tights – whatever you need for it to look complete. If the fit doesn't make you feel like you want to snog the mirror or dry-hump your reflection, return it immediately.

Keep the receipt: How many times have you bought something, loved it and worn it once, only to have it literally fall apart at the seams? It's a downer to have your heart's desire fall to pieces (especially while on your body). It's even worse when you remember you put the receipt into yesterday's recycling run. Keep a special envelope for your clothing receipts and dump after 28 days – never before.

THE BODY SCAN

Sometimes a shopping mission isn't always accomplished. Mirrors mislead us, crowds blind us and our internal GPS leaves us stranded somewhere between our intended target and our best intentions.

The following exercise borrows from the body scan method used in meditation. The idea is to feel how your clothes are fitting by plugging into the sensations that arise from head to toe. We are so used to looking in the mirror, which is loaded with judgement and expectations – not to mention magic shop mirrors that can physically distort our perceptions of how things look. This takes us into a more honest, real place.

Stand tall and close your eyes. Start by focusing your awareness from the top of where the garment touches your body. If you're wearing a hood or a hat, start from the head; otherwise, the neck will do fine. Pay particular attention to any tightness or general sensations in that area.

- Ask yourself how it fits. Do you feel constricted or loose in any area? If so, where?
- Move your arms and legs gently in place. Bend your knees

slightly. How does the fabric feel on your skin? Does it itch, glide, tickle?

- Now ask yourself how it makes you feel. Comfortable, secure, relaxed?

Stand with your eyes closed a little bit longer, shifting your body weight slightly from leg to leg, side to side, all the while keeping your focus on the contact between the skin and the garment. Repeat the same process, concentrating on the sensation of each garment until you reach your toes.

Ultimately, how a garment feels is critical to how it makes you feel about yourself. Sure, it's lovely to have an optical-illusion dress shave a few inches off the waistline – but if you feel like you've been shoved into a medieval torture device, what's the point? Too often we fall foul of bad lighting, wonky sizing or second opinions with a hidden agenda that seem to coincide with moments of weakness and uncertainty. If in doubt, do a mini-meditative barcode scan of your own. No mirror, no queues and no changing room required.

ONLINE SHOPPING

Swipe left, swipe left, swipe left, swipe right. Match! Add to cart. Express shipping (yes, please!). Excitement. Try on. Bad fit. Return. Ring a bell, anyone? You'd be forgiven for not being sure if it's online shopping or online dating in the above scenario. Both have their unique charm (namely variety and convenience), but these same seductive lures do double-time as roadblocks when it comes to forming meaningful relationships.

Think about it:

- Have you ever shopped for new romantic partners/new underwear while you're in bed/on the bus/on the phone to your mother/on the toilet?
- Have you ever experienced the dreaded finger cramp from excessive swiping/scrolling/clicking?
- Have you ever felt deceived by the size or shape of a package when you open it?

Sifting through thousands upon thousands of images, shot professionally and expertly retouched, requires a keen filtering system and oodles of self-discipline. It's very easy to be deceived by a good angle and a flattering filter. It's not quite as easy to achieve a perfect hit-rate, especially when the missing element of touch prevents shoppers from making an instant emotional connection. And remember: you've got a part to play in this as well. Too much of a good thing, as the saying goes, is good for nothing. Not sure what I mean? Think about it some more:

- Do you find yourself shopping for an ego boost/distraction even when you already have enough?
- Do you find yourself constantly looking for something

more attractive or exciting than you already have?
• Do you shop within your type/default when faced with the vastness of choice online?

The glut of choice means we are always looking above our station: why settle on one item when you've got the world of retail at your fingertips? There's also a real danger of cognitive overwhelm, which, as we discovered in Chapter 4, often leads us back to the familiarity of our usual type (€14.99, p+p not included).

In order to achieve lasting closet happiness, you need to engage with the shopping process and give it your full attention. Clicking to cart is just another visual distraction; the cult of newness at work again. It may boost your ego for a moment but as soon as you get bored, you'll be doing the same thing all over again.

And while you can order a pair of kinky boots while you're sunbathing naked in the garden, there's no guarantee you'll like what's inside the delivery man's box when he rings that bell. In fact, it can often be a let-down – and then there's the added hassle of getting dressed and having to return it. If you're happy not to be on first-name terms with the delivery dude, then let's look at nixing those returns and getting a better return on your investment.

Browse	Glance at
Give the once-over	Pass an eye over
Have a butcher's	Dabble
Skim	Glimpse
Scan	Take a gander
Dip into	Have a goo
Once-over lightly	Inspect casually
Skip through	Breeze through

HAPPINESS HACKS

Set your intention: Don't browse. Go online with the intention to find something substantial and concrete. We can be lulled into a false sense of security when shopping from our beds or passing time waiting for our flight or next train. It's remarkably easy to lose four hours of conscious awareness with nothing to show for it. Use it as a tool, not a toy.

Limit your experience: Allow online shopping to be part of your toolkit. The key is to put limits on the usage of online shopping to create a more seamless experience. If you are time-strapped, then it's a godsend but, much like online dating, sometimes the scrolling can be more addictive than the end-game.

Apply the escrow rule: As noted in Chapter 3, Pinterest is a handy half-way house for parking our preferred interests. Many online retailers have wish-lists but Pinterest will collate these wishes collectively. Putting aside anything interesting but unrelated to your shopping mission offsets cognitive overload, which, as we know by now, affects our ability to process information and make decent decisions. Give yourself a cooling-off period of a few days before you click to cart. It's much easier than having to go through the hassle of returns once you've activated that trigger finger.

Fill in the blanks: Shopping from a screen? Without the ability to touch or try on, you're already operating at a loss. With that, reading the fine print is crucial. Most online retailers not only have their own sizing chart but also publish dimensions of the garment and the height and size of their model. Do the maths and scale accordingly. Still unsure? Ask customer service what the fit is like and, where possible, read customer reviews. Most important, familiarise yourself with the returns/exchange policy. Bad fit is a buzzkill; bad terms and conditions are even worse.

There's always a trade-off: Imagine queuing for a changing room with two items. You're told you have to pay upfront before trying anything on. Not everything fits. When you ask the sales assistant for bigger sizes, you're told they don't do exchanges at the moment so you'll have to pay upfront plus handling charges. In the end, you decide to keep just one of the items you've tried, so you return the rest to the sales assistant who informs you that you're obliged to pay a returns charge and, oh, you won't be reimbursed on the others for at least two weeks. You'd probably think twice about using this changing room again, am I right? That's the thing about online shopping – it's conveniently inconvenient. What you gain in instant gratification, you lose in transactional fees and the hassle of returns. That's just the price you pay.

Hedge your bets: Poor fit is one of the biggest reasons cited for online sales returns. Fall between sizes? Split the difference by buying your size plus either a size up or down. Not only will you have a greater chance of getting it right but delivery charges are often waived on larger purchases. That said, you'll probably have to pony up on the returns, but that's the price you pay. See above.

Return it, dammit: 95% of all shoppers cite returns as a barrier to online shopping. Put simply – 95% of all shoppers can't be arsed to return what they buy. Next-day delivery options appear seductive but the implied hassles of sending something back often means we are left with a clanger we don't want – a constant reminder of our wayward decision-making process. Top tip? Return it immediately, or you never will. Why keep something you don't want?

ONLINE SHOPPING CHEATSHEET

Because, every once in a while, cheating is OK.

LOOKING

- Don't shop as a distraction or a salve – make a virtual appointment to shop.
- Don't shop in bed, on the bus or in work.

- Limit your experience – give yourself a timeframe and a mono-task.
- Add items to a wish-list, review then buy.

BUYING

- Read the fine print. Each retailer has their own size.
- Find out what size and height the model is. Scale accordingly.
- Ask customer service what the fit is like.
- Buy your size and the size above or below.
- Buy more than you need.
- Buy more = no shipping charges.
- You will have to pay for returns – but you can do it in one fell swoop.
- Read the returns policy before you buy.
- Read customer reviews.

RETURNING

- Fit is the biggest reason for return.
- You are opcrating on a guesstimate.
- You are operating with sight only – no opportunity to touch or try.
- When you receive the package, try everything on as you would in a shop.
- Return THAT day.
- Do not hesitate or you will not return it. Fact.

KEEPING THE LOVE ALIVE

So you've got it all figured out. You've separated the creepers from the closet-keepers. You've knocked those one-night stands on the head and have taken a more considered approach to style suitors. You're feeling confident. You're looking good. You may even see yourself as a Perfect 9. All is well. For now.

Cast your mind forward a few years. You've grown accustomed to your well-curated closet, so much so that it's more of a background hum than that song that makes you get up and dance. That's what happens in most relationships though, doesn't it? So you don't think about it too much. In fact, you don't think about it at all. Until one day it hits you: you've been wearing the same things in the same way – every day, every year. You feel like you've lost yourself. The thrill is officially gone.

Remember: the very moment you forget that closet happiness is a constantly evolving entity, that's when one of two things will happen:

- You'll grow restless and act out.
- You'll get stuck in a style rut.

Becoming too comfortable in any relationship is a recipe for disaster. And as human beings we're incredibly adept at comfortably adapting to our circumstances. You don't want to ruin a great thing – but you also don't want to let it grow stale. Looking at things with curious eyes allows us an opportunity for creativity and variety, which, in turn, keeps our habits from becoming unconscious or automatic. So what can you do to keep the love alive?

- **Prioritise your closet:** Any relationship worth having takes work. If you want things to go tickety-boo, you'd better prepare to put in the graft. That means regular maintenance, clear-outs, updates and a good dollop of TLC. Taking things for granted only leads to resentment down the road and bouts of 'Why didn't I do this sooner?'

- **Practice preventive care:** There is absolutely zero point in improving the mood of your closet if you are simply going to piss it off in a few months' time by letting it go to pot. Have shoes that could use a spit and polish? Do it before it someone thinks a wild animal has been gnawing at your heels. And as for the saggy elastic in those knickers … I have no words.

- **Do regular date nights:** For every serious clear-out, you should plan an equally fun night of dress-up. Look at what's in your wardrobe and think of new ways to get more mileage out of your visual assets. In the words of designer Karl Lagerfeld, 'Reinvent new combinations of what you already own. Improvise. Become more creative. Not because you have to, but because you want to. Evolution is the secret for the next step.' No one messes with the Kaiser.

- **Stop comparing:** You are the size you are. You are the shape you are. You are the person you are. Start accepting and learning to dress that figure in the mirror instead of the model on the TV advert, your best friend or that girl from work who always seems to get it right. As the old adage goes, 'compare and despair'.

- **Those who stray, pay:** There's a price to be paid for being too comfortable and that's complacency. Before you know it, you'll be throwing shapes at the frilly belly-tops in Forever 21, thinking you actually stand a chance. You can do the decent thing and walk away or risk being blacklisted as a walking mid-life crisis.

In order to really keep the love alive, we need to constantly check in not just with our closets, but with ourselves. Get this relationship right and everything else finds its place. Looks like it's time for an inner selfie.

CHAPTER SEVEN

THE EVOLVING SELF

WHO DO YOU THINK YOU ARE?

'I have already lost touch with a couple of people I used to be.'

JOAN DIDION

The most emotionally draining relationship I've ever had has been with my wardrobe. I spent years trying to win its affection, wondering why it didn't reciprocate, accusing it of untold indiscretions, only to cast it off into black plastic bags and repeat the process over and over again. Figure that one out, Freud.

Had I spent more time learning to acknowledge and appreciate who I really was, much of these flagrant histrionics could have been avoided. Not that the process of self-realisation was a cake walk, mind you.

Despite shedding the vestiges of my assumed identity (reigning fashion editor living the high life), I had yet to master dressing the real me (fashion editor living where it rains). In short, I looked a state.

For each step forward, I took three staggering backwards into past habits. I knew that if I were to cultivate any sense of awareness, I had to get to grips with the earlier versions of my 'self' so that I could figure out how and why I was getting so stuck.

With that, I took a trip down memory lane and had rather revealing 'Do you remember when?' chats with some very honest friends. The end result? I quit playing the fashion victim and became the leading lady in my own story again.

After all, who wants to be a fashion victim? It's just a colourful idiom for 'clueless' – speaking somebody else's words, following somebody else's script. The moment you create a persona, that person you think you should play, is the very moment you lose direction – the moment you lose the plot.

To help you find your inner story and discover your leading lady, I've put together an exercise that will help you understand and reconnect with the past selves that have shaped who you are today. See it as a school reunion without the fake smiles, name badges and dodgy punch – and, more important, without having to compare yourself to others. The past is worthwhile insofar as it gives context to the present but we don't want to live there. A bit like any trip down memory lane, this visit should be brief and the reminiscing should be minimal. Tired & Emotional and Martyr Mom, pay attention. We want you back in one piece.

Think about it. Who were you five, ten, fifteen years ago? Did you have the same job? Perhaps you're living in a different country; maybe you've had kids – triplets even? Have you gone from corporate banker to kitchen start-up? Lost two stone? Gained two stone? Got a boob job?

Although our personalities are not subject to radical change, the circumstances surrounding them are forever protean, little shapeshifters that radically alter the landscape of how we dress.

Using the chart on pages 186–7 as a guideline, map out the trajectory of your life every five or so years from the age of 18, paying special attention to your biggest life and personal challenges.

Why 18? For many of us, it's a coming of-age, that generational gear shift where we start taking respons bility for our choices: which college to attend, job to accept, road to take. With choices come changes; with changes come plot twists. If you want to transition from victim to hero, then you'd best get extra familiar with your character arc – the flaws and strengths that drive your personal narrative.

Once you've dished the details, read each section out loud. Be sure to refer to yourself in the third person. This will distance yourself from the narrative and allow you to form an objective conclusion as to where the conflict has been playing out and how to resolve it. Repeat this for each section until you start to understand where your closet is getting stuck.

For example:

Aoife was living alone in London when she was 25. The biggest turning point in her life was the birth of her first child. Her personal challenge was trying to balance work and home life. She didn't sleep much and put her own personal needs on the back-burner. She was still living in London when she was 30, now as a single parent. The biggest turning points in her life were her daughter going to school and losing the three stone she gained since Ella was born. Her personal challenge was trying to get her head to catch up with her body. She still wore her old maternity clothes and baggy tops from five years ago because she wasn't body confident, nor was she confident about how to dress her new shape.

I've plotted my own story in the chart overleaf. In retelling my own narrative, I began to notice the area that had the biggest influence on my sartorial undoing – my career. Not knowing what I wanted to do, I was literally trying on jobs for about ten years (not counting bouts of temping, bar jobs and nixers). With that came the radical swings from corporate suits to media middle youth. When I finally got the courage to follow my heart's desire, I thought I had to 'be' a certain way. It's with the help of this exercise that I came to understand who I really am. Let's see if you can do the same.

WHAT'S YOUR STORY?

'You gotta know yourself very well, and you have to be honest with what you can pull off. If you're not comfortable with it, no matter how marvellous the outfit is, you're gonna look like a jerk, because you're gonna be so uncomfortable.'

IRIS APFEL

My Fashion Phases

Grace Jones meets Cistercian monk – buzz cut, hoods, lots of draping

Queen of the Romulan Empire –space age shoulder pads, weaponry jewellery

Jackie O, the Hyannis Port Years – popped collars, Capri pants

Curtis Mayfield and Cher have a Love Child – velvet, flares, inflated hair

The Matrix Reloaded – leather, PVC, sunglasses

Unwitting Hipster – beanie, PLO scarf, coffee

This Old Thing? – vintage, charity shop, hand-me-down

Utility Chic – boilersuits, heels, prodigious furs

Elvis Joins the Military – quiff, army jackets, cowboy boots

Come On Eileen – built-ups, brogues, no socks

Hamlet does McQueen – skulls, lots of skulls

Extreme Sports – vertiginous heels, heavy-as-hell handbags

Kids' TV Presenter – fluoro brights, braces, arm warmers

Girl Band Auditionee – parachute pants, shrunken tank tops, trainers

Gold Digger in Training – designer dress, empty wallet

The Mr T Appreciation Society – chunky chains, lots of chunky chains

Pick that Winkle, Why Don't You? – brothel creepers, stilettos, spikes and studs

My Story

AGE	18	22	25	30	35	40
LOCATION	Athenry	Bologna	Monza	London	Dublin	Dublin
JOB	Student	Student	English teacher	Radio sales and freelance journalist	Freelance journalist, blogger and stylist	Freelance journalist, stylist and soon-to-be-published author
LIVING ARRANGEMENTS	At home with my mother and four sisters	In a studio apartment with my flatmate and sometimes her extended Calabrian family	In an apartment with four other teachers	In a Victorian conversion with three other girls	Living alone in a rented house	Went from living alone to moving in with my sister, from city centre to suburbs
KIDS/NO KIDS	No kids	No kids	No kids	No kids	Two part-time cats	No cats – they sodded off
TYPICAL CLOTHING	School uniform	Full-on fashion gale-force wind (the experimental years)	Suits to work, Brit Pop retro streetwear for play	Tank tops, parachute pants, Adidas trainers and denim jacket	Leather, spikes – anything that made me feel like the woman I was pretending to be	Lots of colour and softer silhouettes

AGE	18	22	25	30	35	40
PHYSICAL APPEARANCE	Size 12–14	Size 10 (the poverty diet)	Size 12–14	Size 12	Size 12	Size 12
	Mid-length curly brown hair	Long curly brown hair	Long curly brown hair	Short black straight hair with micro fringe	Really short straight black hair with Elvis quiff	Long chestnut brown hair with highlights and greys that need tending every fortnight!
BIGGEST LIFE CHANGES	Passing my Leaving Cert	Moving to a different country with no knowledge of the language	Figuring out what to do with my life	Figuring out what to do with my life	Working for myself and creating a successful business; starting a blog that helped me achieve that	Got the book deal I've wanted for so long – official author
PERSONAL CHALLENGES	Planning a life outside secondary school	Passing my exams in a different language	Not getting fired; not killing my flatmates; not running out of money before month's end	Not getting fired; not killing my flatmates; not running out of money before month's end	Maintaining relationships while chasing invoices, chasing work, chasing my tail	Moving house; helping my sister deal with the death of her best friend; putting other people ahead of me

THROUGH THE LOOKING GLASS

'It's no use to go back to yesterday because I was a different person then.'

LEWIS CARROLL, *ALICE IN WONDERLAND*

I'm not a fan of approval by committee. Rarely does it serve the individual, even if the consensus is a thumbs-up. External validation may give the ego a much-loved boost but too much of a good thing can interfere with the ability to choose rather than be chosen. That being said, every once in a while, it's helpful to integrate the impressions of others, if only to get a less one-sided and more public view of our image.

Whether we care to admit it or not, reflected appraisals do account for much of how we view ourselves. Psychologist Charles Horton, who created the concept of the 'looking glass self', maintains that our identities develop through the perceptions of others – namely, the circles of friends and acquaintances with whom we surround ourselves. Indeed, the beauty of the looking glass circle of friends is that they upend our stale perceptions of ourselves and give them a ruddy good shake. There's nothing like a shot of honesty serum to challenge the status quo but, as you know by now, the brain isn't fond of too much challenge. Pity, that. We've got a juicy one coming right up!

For this exercise, I want you to park your ego. In fact, hand over the keys while you're at it. You'll need:

- An open mind
- A handful of honest friends
- A glass of wine to take the edge off (*go on, I'll let you*).

If you're the sensitive type, this is probably best executed over email rather than on the phone or face-to-face. There's nothing worse than getting the gang over for a few bevvies and a game of truth when the subject of the day is how you dress. Makes it a tad awkward when the *vino* and the *veritas* clash.

Start with a straw poll of your closest friends and family and ask them how they would describe your fashion identity (how you *appear* to them) using the phrase 'You're the kind of person who …'

Here's the twist: using the self-knowledge you've accrued in What's Your Story?, get them to describe you THEN (five years ago, ten years ago) and NOW. See how their answers compare to yours but be ready to accept their answers – good or bad.

Here's an example of my own:

Katherine

NOW: You're the kind of person who … is comfortable in her own skin, knows what suits her and, as a consequence, always looks beautiful.

THEN: You're the kind of person who … wanted to be someone

else. Although you had a very edgy, coherent look, it wasn't really you. Sometimes we all want to play dress-up but it can't be the foundation of our whole aesthetic.

Neil

NOW: You're the kind of person who … instinctively knows what style works for them and doesn't obsess about following trends: your style is a reflection of you, not the other way around.

THEN: You're the kind of person who … enjoyed wedging themselves into thigh-high purple snakeskin boots and then insisting your friends carried them when you could no longer walk at 3 a.m., while flagging down a taxi.

Margaret

NOW: You're the kind of person who … has an immediately recognisable signature style: elegant with a bit of edge. I know exactly who you are just by looking at you.

THEN: You're the kind of person who … had a different look for every day. Often I wasn't sure which Annmarie would show up. Although you were brave enough to try everything, you never really settled on anything.

Bang on the money. Their feedback served to confirm my own feelings on the matter: the less I tried to be someone I wasn't, the easier it became to understand who I was. Simplicity at its best.

The trick is not to rely solely on the validation of others (I'm looking at you, Impulse Buyer) or to be so caught up in the idea of 'you' that you fail to see another perspective (hello, Perfect 9!). Self-serving biases do nothing but air-kiss our egos, which, by the way, are still parked and under lock and key, so don't go there. Allowing external views to gently balance our self-perceptions will help us come to a more level appraisal of how we appear. That's when we can focus on what to keep, what to tweak and – the part hated by most – what to let go.

IMPLEMENTING CHANGE

So what's the next step if you want to implement any changes? According to James Clear, author of *Transform Your Habits*, in order to create new behaviours we need to focus first on creating a new identity. A big ask, but the man's got a point.

Our current habits, Clear maintains, reflect the person we think we are (whether consciously or subconsciously). So if you want an organised, planned and unified wardrobe or the ability to pack a 10-kilo case for a two-week trip in ten minutes, then you have to prove it to yourself first. In other words, the actions you take and the perceptions of others can motivate you to change, but the only way it will stick is if you commit to the belief that the change is possible.

In my case, I identified the personal challenge in my story, corroborated the evidence with my peers and took steps to create a more cohesive visual front, but I left out the most important part – belief. Niggling insecurities compounded by a lingering whiff of self-doubt left me in limbo. In theory, I understood I *could be* strong and understated, minimalist with maximum impact – I just had to know I *was* that person.

Trust me, this took a while – which is why you'll need to draw on your signature style from Chapter 5 if you want to manifest a similar reality for yourself.

Remember? Fresh, colourful, sleek? Poised, urban, effortless? Repeat your signature style until it is tattooed on your subconscious. Then start owning it by pinning those three magic words onto the phrase 'I am the kind of person who is … ' Ready?

I AM THE KIND OF PERSON WHO IS FRESH, COLOURFUL AND SLEEK.

Aaaaand one more time – with feeling.

I AM THE KIND OF PERSON WHO IS FRESH, COLOURFUL AND SLEEK.

The subconscious mind is mightily receptive to repetition (think back to those multiplication tables from your school days) and a bit gullible to boot. Tell it a few porkie pies (good or bad) and it will begin to believe them. So even if your closet looks like it was put together by your colour-blind arch-nemesis in a drunken fit of pique, fake it 'til you make it.

So what if you get it wrong along the way? The more you make it your practice, the closer you'll get to perfecting it. Put down the bulletproof vest. Stop creating an armour against the outside world. Instead, find those pieces that make you vulnerable – that expose the real you. Yes, it's scary baring your soul but if you don't show people who you really are, how will you ever know yourself?

IF THE SHOE DOESN'T FIT ...

When I was young, I was alleged to have thrown epic tantrums when taken to get new shoes. This may have had to do with being measured by a stranger with a 'Hi, Can I Help You?' badge at Long Island's Start Rite or the fact that my mother, ever the practical soul, would insist on buying mine a size bigger so that I'd grow into them. I must have had some precognition that my freakish growing foot was only getting started and so the theatrics began.

I would throw myself prostrate on the floor like Maria Callas in a rendition of *Tosca* as my mortified mother attempted to retrieve my flailing body. Let's not mention the time I flung a pair of sensible sandals at my aunt after she dared to call them 'pretty'. The poor woman.

Fast-forward to my prodigious adult size 8 feet and hey ho waddayaknow, getting 'pretty' shoes is about as easy as singing a verse of 'Vedi, ecco, vedi' backwards. Finding my lesser-spotted size in anything other than a sneaker, boot or something resembling a canal boat is about as hopeless as hoping to bump into Sasquatch having a beer in your local. So throughout my 20s (and 30s), denial was my constant companion.

Rather than save my feet from a life of bunions and pinched nerves, I succumbed to the 'too pretty to pass up' excuse and shoved my hooves into the daintiest and highest pairs of heels I could find. Invariably, these were one or even two sizes too small and frequently too tight (did I mention my feet are also wide?). Despite experiencing toe overhang and an unsightly case of foot muffin-top in anything vaguely open or strappy, I'd persist rather than resist, with denial always at my side with a ration of rational lies: 'It'll be grand'; 'Honestly, you can't notice'; 'Of course you can walk in those!'

Without fail, I'd manage a few wears before relegating them to the back of my wardrobe. Now and again, I'd take them out, try them on and stare longingly in the mirror as if my abject looks of despair would somehow make them expand in sympathy. Much to my own mortification, it wasn't until I was 38 and lost the feeling in my left thigh due to a trapped nerve caused by wearing heels that I got some sense.

Go ahead, say it. 'You big fool!' I couldn't agree more. This is what happens, folks, when the ego takes the wheel.

Self-acceptance gets the bum's rush and before you can say tendonitis, you're selling your soles to the devil. My point? Never buy what doesn't fit. Ever.

Whether a shoe, a hat, a dress or anything, really – if you can't wear it right now, how is it supposed to make you or your closet happy? Go back to your closet mantra. Does it make you look relevant, put-together and current? If you can't answer 'yes' to all three of your closet mantra words, then walk away (or hobble, in my case).

It's a bit like buying a plane ticket for a holiday you can't take. Simply printing out that boarding pass won't get you to Malaga, so what's the point? If you do feel compelled to sit in the departures lounge and watch those Ryanair flights take off, try implementing one of the tips below or, at the very least, think of the hefty fine you'd be smacked with for sneaking denial on board.

HAPPINESS HACKS

Stay present: Unless you are already taking steps to diet into those size 10 jeans, keeping them is preventing you from engaging with the now. By focusing on what doesn't fit, you avoid having to deal with what's real. Appearance-based habits, according to James Clear, only motivate us once they are in operation (think of how hard it is to get to the gym but how pumped you feel once you've finished your workout). Otherwise, they simply serve as a mockery, a reminder of our failed choices.

Good for: All closet types

Don't deny it: Numbers carry serious weight. Even the smallest fluctuation – whether our bank accounts or dress size – can send us into a mind-funk. Fluctuations happen – that's life. And if genes have their way, sometimes there's sod-all we can do about it. Denial is simply an insidious form of self-rejection. Don't like what it says on the tag? That's what scissors are for …

Good for: All closet types

What's so uncomfortable? Mastering a choke-hold on the past won't stop it from being past tense. It'll just stop you from dealing with uncomfortable feelings – apart from the hand cramp you're bound to be feeling right now. When we can't let go of the past, there's often an unresolved fear afoot. That ex you can't get over? It's not him you crave; it's the security of a relationship and your fear of not finding another. Those skin-tight leather trousers that no longer fit? Don't hold a funeral for your mojo just yet. Feeling sexy comes from within, so get in touch with your inner vixen. Besides, she needs the support. There's some rumour doing the rounds that she popped her clogs.

Good for: Tired & Emotional

CORE CLOSET VALUES (CCV)

'When a woman says, "I have nothing to wear!", what she really means is, "There's nothing here for who I'm supposed to be today."'

CAITLIN MORAN, *HOW TO BE A WOMAN*

FIRE! There's a fire and it's happening in your wardrobe! NOW!

– STOP –

What's the first image that comes to mind?

Your wedding dress charred beyond recognition?

Those Japanese selvedge jeans reduced to a pile of cinders?

60 pairs of flaming shoes being hurled out of a window?

Whether it's a keepsake or an old reliable with an incomparable cost-per-wear ratio, the things that have us dialling 999 are those through which we determine the true value of our wardrobe. The prospect of loss has a unique way of concentrating the mind, which comes in handy when you find yourself moaning, 'I have nothing to wear.' Simply shout 'FIRE!' and you'll soon find out what you really value. Shout too loudly, though, and you'll wind up frightening the neighbours, so perhaps a less vocal assessment is in order?

Decisions, Decisions, Decisions

Let's start with understanding what your closet priorities. By becoming more conscious of what you expect from your clothing, you will be better positioned to make informed shopping decisions and manage the lingering spectre of regret. Let's face it, many of our decisions in life are really about determining what we prioritise most. Why should our wardrobes be any different?

For example, if you value comfort but have a wardrobe filled with tight, body-conscious dresses, will you feel satisfied? Equally, if you value ornate and visually stimulating pieces, will a rack of minimalist separates really do it for you?

We are at our happiest when our personal value system is in alignment with our actions. We may get giddy with excitement at having broken the back of our new credit card on a slinky dress but the high garnered from material goods plateaus after a period of time. If you're looking for a longer-term connection with what you wear, it needs to come from a deeper tether, not just surface value.

Using the chart opposite, make a list of those items that give you the most bang for your buck on an emotional and a practical level. If you're scratching your head, take a gander back at Question 12 in Chapter 1's Closet Quiz: your highest cost-per-wear and your happiest purchases.

Next, describe the feeling you associate with each one. A leather jacket may make you feel invincible, put-together or bodacious like Boudicca. Your skinny jeans could do the same. It's OK if there's overlap. In fact, it's more than OK – it's great. What we're looking here for are word patterns. Once you've filled in the blanks, highlight those feelings that repeat themselves.

My Core Closet Values

ITEM	FEELING
Leather joggers	Easy-to-wear, durable, versatile (wear with everything and anything – like upscale tracksuit bottoms!)
Single-breasted wool coat	Easy-to-wear, smart, versatile (can wear with jeans or a dress)
Leather (double handle) day bag	Durable, smart, versatile (extra cross-body handle makes it doubly practical)
Cashmere sweater	Versatile, feminine, smart (goes with everything, can wear in any season)
Jersey pencil skirt with slit in front	Feminine, smart, easy-to-wear (wash-and-wear, slit makes it easy to walk)
Perspex high heels	Durable (never had to get them reheeled in five years), feminine, smart
Reebok retro trainers	Easy-to-wear, durable (bung them into the wash), versatile (can wear with skirts or leather joggers)

Looking at my list, the key words that emerge for me are: feminine, easy-to-wear, durable, versatile and smart.

Now it's time to break out that diary again and find yours.

When you go shopping or clear your closet, ensure that each item ticks at least three of your CCV words. Having this tool in your back pocket also proves its worth when cross-checking the integrity behind our choices – in other words, it will knock any shady excuses or rational lies squarely on the head.

Those strappy stilettoes you love may be feminine but are they also easy-to-wear and versatile? If it takes a degree in engineering to strap them on or if you can only wear them with the help of three assistants and a wire rope pulley, a more suitable alternative might be in order. That goes double for decluttering. Sometimes the prospect of starting everything all over again is too much to think about. Throwing things out is tantamount to rescinding parts of your identity. But by using this tool, the process of clearing and curating will become a habit worth forming.

WHAT YOU CAN GAIN BY LETTING GO

'Cultivate the habit of making aware choice. Your choice makes your destiny.'

AMIT RAY

2 garden chairs (broken)

golf clubs (not mine)

Christmas decorations

CD compilations

1 sink

2008–2013 tax receipts

picture frames

college notes

VCR tapes

floppy disks

snow globe

flip-flops (8 pairs)

wrapping paper

weighing scales

mosquito net

more Christmas decorations

old sheets

lace doilies

charity bracelets

newspaper cuttings

bikinis

snow boots (3 pairs)

galoshes

DVD player

1 lawnmower

Margaret Thatcher coffee-table
book

Wi-Fi keyboard (still in box)

blankets

wicker basket

1994–1996 personal diaries (the
Galway years)

ballcock

some wire

Crocs (definitely not mine)

sleeping bag

60-litre rucksack

Santa bear

photograph negatives

17 chargers

S-bend pipe

jar of buttons

3 kettles (all broken)

bag of necklaces (all broken)

lampshade

hand weights (never used)

skipping rope (definitely never
used)

25 reusable shopping bags

Venetian mask

box of bathroom tiles

Betamax cassette (*Under Siege*
starring Steven Seagal)

AS ABOVE, SO BELOW

I recently moved house. I'd love to tell you that I found the process cathartic or that I had a moment of self-discovery. Sadly, the only thing I discovered is that I'm a total fraud. Mounting my soapbox and preaching the mantra of mindfulness, I open my wardrobe and bare my soul to anyone who'll stand there long enough to listen to my self-styled philosophy of conscious sartorial awareness. Amid the boxes, bubble wrap, and packing tape, I congratulated myself for mastering my historic hoarding impulses. I had it nailed – that is, until I opened the attic ...

Much like the magic satchels that occupy the fantasy narrative of video games and sci-fi novels, that small portal in the ceiling harboured my own raw materials for the game of life. Deep within her panelled hammer-space recesses lay remnants of past selves, future promises and classified information (namely, receipts) tucked artfully away from public scrutiny. She was my dirty secret and, boy, did she have the goods on me. I winced at the thought of how I was going to transfer this arsenal of stuff through a two-foot wide opening – and, more to the point, how did I ever get it up there in the first place?

Truth be told, I couldn't recall the genesis of most of this junk. Sifting through the detritus, something struck me. Not one thing in this raftered space occupied the present tense; all that existed was past and future. Nostalgia commingled with potential (old college notes, unused jump ropes) with no sense of the current moment. Was I really ever going to revisit my '90s shorthand on Medieval Aesthetics? Did I really intend to commit to 700 skips per day in a bid to lose a pound of fat a week? I felt like *Harry Potter*'s Hermione Granger, conjuring a library full of books and a tent from a beaded velvet pouch, albeit with much less fanfare. Everything I had that occupied the now was already loaded into a transit van. Had it not been for a timely reminder from my sister, I most likely would have forgotten I even had an attic.

Whether I chose to acknowledge it or not, the crawl space was more than just a dumping ground; it was a not-so-shiny citadel to my unconscious hopes and fears. The hodgepodge of bits and bobs was a pitiable extension of my unacknowledged need for security. Sure, I had my closet sorted but that fear of loss – in particular, losing my identity amid the chaos of moving from London back to Dublin almost ten years ago – still lingered. Unconsciously, I was keeping back-up as emotional ballast. It wasn't that I needed a Betamax copy of *Under Siege* to feel secure (even with Steven Seagal as action hero); but keeping it made me feel settled in some strange way, as if having this weight would prevent my world being rocked, yet again.

But why did I need a Betamax copy of *Under Siege* to feel a tether to the past? Why did I need to cart that all the way over from London (I found my moving boxes from 2006, immaculately preserved)? Items give us a sense of stability in an otherwise chaotic world. I buy, therefore I am. I have, therefore

I am. Seeing things out of context (not on bookshelves or hangers) made them look less appealing and made me question the 'why' behind my motives. When forced to look at what we've accumulated, there's an attendant twang of guilt for having squandered money on junk and having nothing to show for it. As a result, we keep the offending articles rather than get rid of them, almost to pseudo-justify our errant ways and not feel so naked. The trick in knowing the difference between keepsakes and keeping something for the sake of it. Need some help? Apply the Keep or Cull Audit.

THE KEEP OR CULL AUDIT

Everyone's got an attic of shoulda, woulda, coulda. The trick to distilling these down to what really matters lies in a few simple questions. By way of illustration, I'm comparing my *Under Siege* Betamax cassette to my late father's Claddagh ring. The words 'no comparison' come to mind, am I right? Wrong. Emotions, being the energy balls that they are, regularly short-circuit the channels of logic. How else can we explain one-night stands, One Direction or one size fits all? Suddenly, *Under Siege* takes on the cinematic grandeur of *The Killing Fields* and before you know it, you're sending that clunky plastic B-rate beauty by air courier, only to leave it in an attic for nine years and then (almost) repeat the same action ... yet again. Bad decisions happen despite our best efforts but the Keep or Cull Audit, a simple mindfulness exercise, can go a long way to breaking bad and creating life-long habits that lead to closet happiness.

Does it bring me happiness?
Claddagh ring: Always. It is my most prized possession.
Under Siege: Only insofar as recounting the final fictional voyage of America's mightiest battleship usurped by a team of terrorists can bring you joy.

Does it currently enhance my life? If so, how?
Claddagh ring: It is a beautiful reminder of my father.
Under Siege: It does not. I can catch it on *Netflix* if I ever feel the need.

How did this come into my life?
Claddagh ring: My mother gave me this ring as a Christmas gift when I was 14.
Under Siege: I won this as a booby prize captaining the worst-performing team at our local pub quiz.

Why am I keeping this?
Claddagh ring: I am keeping this to pass on to future generations.
Under Siege: Good question. If for nothing else, Seagal sounds like a damn fine catch. 'Ryback is an ex-SEAL, expert in martial arts, explosives, weapons and tactics and recipient of the Silver

Star, Navy Cross and Purple Heart. He also cooks.' Swipe right on that Tinder blurb, why dontcha?

Does it have a decent resale value?
Claddagh ring: It is more a family heirloom than potential collateral.
Under Siege: Currently €4.13 on eBay.

Has it been passed down through the generations?
Claddagh ring: Passed to me from my father, it will hopefully pass to many generations to come.
Under Siege: I am the first, of no generations to come.

Would my future kin be pleased if it were passed on to them?
Claddagh ring: I should hope so; it is very special.
Under Siege: I should hope not.

Does it have a future purpose?
Claddagh ring: Its very presence is itself purpose.
Under Siege: A doorstop? Coaster? Hipster paraphernalia?

Letting go doesn't mean giving up. Quite the opposite. It means allowing new energy and new life into your closet. Remember what was said in Chapter 1?

The easiest way to manage choice (and its kissing cousin, regret) is in knowing who you are.

The act of holding on to clothes that no longer serve you subconsciously allows you to fall back into old habits. Denial is more than just sticking your head in the sand; it's preventing you from real growth. Holding on to things that simply don't fit – be it our bodies or our current lifestyle – makes a mockery of who we are today.

Creating an honest interior inventory is key to improving the exterior. As within, so without. Real and honest change can only manifest when we give it space – lots of space. Get ready to clear the decks. We've got some decluttering to do.

CHAPTER EIGHT

CLEARING THE SPACE FOR CHANGE

TACKLING PROCRASTINATION

'Procrastination is the art of keeping up with yesterday.'

DON MARQUIS

S o you're ready to face your demons. I guess it's time to make a cup of tea. Oh, and don't forget to change the ringtone on your phone. Have you fed the cat? You have. Well, feed the dog then. While you're at it, have you seen that cute kitten meme on BuzzFeed? Turn up the radio. This is a great tune. Did someone say something about demons? I can't hear anything with all this noise.

There's nothing like a healthy dose of distraction to put off the inevitable. Despite the mounting evidence (burgeoning clothing heaps, growing inertia, the smell of despair), there's always a good reason to avoid tackling a closet clear-out. Why? Because it's bloody exhausting, that's why.

The strict focus required to bridge the gap between starting and finishing (as Rolf Dobelli explains in *The Art of Thinking Clearly*) is such that it literally drains our willpower – and once mental energy is compromised, that's when we jack it all in to watch two series of *Breaking Bad* back-to-back. Unless there's something a bit deeper than an energy slump afoot. If you are still coming up with creative 'reasons' for delaying the inevitable, it's best to check in with how you're feeling.

Much of our procrastination isn't based on having better things to do ('better' does not include 'more entertaining') but rather on more latent underlying fears: fear of what lies ahead, fear of the mess we've made, fear of our next-level regret. It's no wonder then that procrastination has its own addictive appeal.

Putting things on pause may make us feel better in the short term by lowering tension and easing anxiety but it can greatly impact our long-term well-being. So instead of brewing yourself another cuppa, why not discover what's behind this brewing unease. Can you answer 'yes' to any of the following questions?

- Do you feel guilt or shame about how much money you've wasted on unworn clothes?
- Are you embarrassed about the catastrophic state of your closet?
- Does the size of the task fill you with anxiety?
- Are you afraid of how getting rid of things will make you feel?

If so, it's time to absolve yourself of your closet sins. You heard me. A bit of self-compassion is in order. Why be so hard on yourself? It happens to all of us. You're not alone. Now, do you feel better? You should.

According to Dr Kelly McGonigal, health psychologist, lecturer at Stanford University and author of *Maximum*

Willpower, forgiveness increases accountability and makes us less likely to continue the pattern of procrastination. Why? McGonigal maintains it takes away the shame and pain of thinking about what has happened in the past and makes us more likely to receive advice from others and learn from the experience. The mental whips of self-criticism simply serve to create more stress, driving us into the arms of what she rightly terms 'comfort coping'. Want to procrastinate more, do a bit more impulse-shopping, make more excuses? Then keep beating yourself up. You're doing a great job. Want to get started on some closet decluttering? Then let it go and get to work. You've got some ghostbusting to do.

HAPPINESS HACKS

Fight brain drain: Keep snacks, water and juice to hand and refuel at regular two-hour intervals. Be sure to stop for a decent lunch break too. The trick to sustaining and completing a task as emotionally charged as weeding your wardrobe boils down to something quite simple – blood sugar. Without regularly replenishing glucose levels, willpower will dry up like a pre-packaged boy band after three songs. Suddenly, deciding whether to bin that shirt with the cigarette burns will seem a cognitive feat too far. Decision fatigue will set in and the whole process will grind to an unceremonious halt. And to think, all you needed was a biscuit.

Take a break: Starting to flag? Take two minutes to stretch your legs, throw water on your face, cry – whatever you need to do. Just give yourself a timeframe and get back to business. Although distractions can be detrimental, small breaks are known to improve decision-making and performance. Studies show that the unconscious mind continues to actively work out problems even while the conscious mind is engaged in a different activity (those ah-ha! moments generally come when the mind and body are taking five).

Ditch distractions: Clear your diary. Feed and water all dependants, then deposit them with whomever or whatever will look after them for the course of a day – child-minder, pet-sitter, football match. Turn off the TV, radio, laptop and your smartphone. Better yet, give your phone to a friend, partner or sibling who will do PA duties for the day. Otherwise, you'll only wind up playing Candy Crush Saga in a moment of weakness.

No alcohol: Leave the glass of vino until the project has been completed. As tempting as it may be to lift your spirit with a tipple of Tempranillo, this is not the time to soften your mental guard. Alcohol reduces our glucose levels, which, in turn, affects our willpower and self-control. Before you know it, you'll be on a mercy mission to save that Carmen Miranda ra-ra skirt from certain death. Don't do it. Just don't.

Bring in the recruits: This is not a job to be tackled alone. Grab an objective third party to help make executive decisions (that frank friend with no filter will do nicely once again), fill those black plastic bags and top up that mug of tea. Treat your friend like a pair of training wheels on a bike: their support helps you stop wobbling and falling off but once you achieve a certain rhythm and confidence, you'll be able to steer your course alone.

Break it down: Have more than three wardrobes? Stuff stashed in the attic? What about the garden shed? Calculate your estimated closet inventory by the amount of time needed to clear it, e.g. 4 hours per closet x 3 closets = 12 hours plus breaks. That's an entire weekend or one closet per night for three allocated nights of the week. I advocate the latter.

Easy does it: Most productivity blogs and gurus advocate starting strong and knocking difficult tasks on the head first. I say pish posh. The willpower required to tackle a project as emotionally loaded as closet decluttering is enough to have you give up midway and commit to a life of chaos. Procrastination, like denial, is merely another coping mechanism to help us deal with the anxiety associated with starting or completing any task or decision. Neil Fiore, author of *The Now Habit*, suggests punctuating small periods of work with regular breaks and rewards. Now that's my kind of advice, if for no other reason than it works with the brain's natural inclinations (pleasure over pain). The mental discomfort of contemplating a full day's decluttering is easily up there with a root canal (hold the anaesthetic) for some people.

Face the bogeyman: Hoarding is often linked to a sense of vulnerability and, to a certain degree, self-blame. So, you haven't done a proper clear-out since 1998. And so what, you spent a small mortgage on shoes that still have the swing tags intact. Will the world come to an end because of it? Nah. What's behind those wardrobe doors often isn't as scary as you think. Face your fears; don't feed them.

Put it in reverse: Suffering from closet overwhelm? The 'Reverse Calendar', a super tip in *The Now Habit*, puts the focus on the present moment, thus easing the anxiety of completing a large and looming task. By working backwards in increments from a planned deadline, the brain's attention is placed mindfully on the immediate undertaking. As more focused energy leads to better results, the process is more enjoyable and less stressful.

THE DECLUTTERING EMOTIONAL ARC

The process of decluttering can trigger some extreme emotions – fear, loss, shame, guilt. It can also make you feel like a rockstar bad-ass superhero capable of taking on the world and its mother (that bit generally comes at the end). The beginning and middle are often more complex. Here's what you can expect.

Procrastination
Tomorrow is another day. And the day after that. And the day after that …

Trepidation
I'm so afraid of what I'll find. What will I find? WHAT WILL I FIND?!

Motivation

You know, this isn't so bad after all. It's actually kind of therapeutic.

Realisation

My closet is really bare. It's REALLY bare. IT'S REALLY BARE!

Compensation

Look, I'll just keep these 65 things. The rest can go.

Integration

OK. Weak moment. Forget I said that. I suppose it's best to keep going until it's finished.

Celebration

Hurrah! I can see the carpet again. It's blue? *Really?* Since when?

CLEARING YOUR CLOSET: THE CLOSET NCT – DECIDING WHAT STAYS AND WHAT GOES

Now that we've got an insight into the mechanics of what drives you, it's time to look at the nuts and bolts of your closet. Whether you shop like time and space are about to collapse or, indeed, if the thought of shopping makes *you* want to collapse, we've got to assess the vehicle before we can tune it up. Got it? Good. Now hand over the keys.

Closet NCT: Annual test of wardrobe worthiness, general cohesion and signs of sartorial exhaustion required for any collection of clothing over three years old as defined in the *Closet Cop-on Act 2015*. The test is self-regulating and covers the following aspects:

- **Suspension:** Are your knickers in good nick? No garment, however expensive, ever looked the part without some decent shock absorbers. Get properly measured for bras every six months (hormones + age = shape change). Thongs, briefs, tangas or shapewear: whatever your preference, please ensure adequate fit and coverage. Nothing looks worse than VPL or someone's arse cheeks taking their cotton briefs hostage.

- **Steering:** These drivers give direction to your wardrobe. Whatever your lifestyle (soccer mom, Cirque du Soleil performer, dominatrix), the contents of your closet should be held together by those pieces worn most regularly. Not a day goes by without a gimp mask and latex teddy? Then make sure they occupy at least 60% of your closet space. Leave the other 40% for special occasions, off-duty apparel, trends and season-specific wear. Everything else must go.

- **Bodywork:** Structure trumps trends. Hormones, babies, genes, age and cream cakes have all conspired to make us feel insecure about at least one body part, especially when the words 'tight' or 'short' crop up. Valuing cut and silhouette over fashion helps alleviate any muffin top/ squishy thighs/wonky boob (delete as necessary) angst.

Throw out anything that gives you insecurity – namely, any offending article that requires tugging, pulling, praying, rib bruising or vital organ compression in order to fit.

- **Accessories:** Scarves, jewellery, belts, gloves – anything that pulls the old switcheroo and makes people think they haven't seen the same outfit twice is a keeper. Bags, however, require more room. Unless you've got a display unit or some savvy Swedish space-saving mechanism, they will multiply in ways that will mess with your head and swallow your keys. Be ruthless. Implement a rule of thumb – only what fits on the shelf, only what won't warrant a new extension or divorce proceedings – and stick to it.

- **Tyres and wheels:** Sort out chewed heels, scuff-marks and peeling soles and replace insoles. Any shoes that hurt, pinch or cause irreparable joint damage should be considered a potential safety risk. Avoid being a statistic by applying the following formula designed to determine your individual maximum heel height (Institute of Physics: London, UK): $h = Q \cdot (12 + 3s / 8)$.

The quantum mechanics, based on Pythagoras's theorem, takes into account variables such as shoe size, 'pull' factor, cost, years of experience, fashionability and alcohol consumption. According to the Institute of Physics, a size 6 heel-wearer with five years' experience in tottering around on their toes can, when sober, handle a 5-inch heel on their new-season Louboutins. However, if she consumes six units of alcohol, ¾ of an inch is a much safer bet – the lower the heel, the lower the face-to-pavement risk.

- **Lighting:** Pick a colour scheme. There's no point in throwing effort and hard-earned cash at a closet that looks like a unicorn's hen party. Apply the same principle as you would to decorating a home: stick to two main hues and two accents as the core basics and scale outwards from there.

- **Mirrors:** Invest in a full-length mirror. Editing clothes only works when you can see how a garment hangs on your body. Jumping up and down to glimpse the back of your arse in those trousers or balancing Twister-like on a chair to assess that skirt-and-heel combo is not only dangerous but stupid. This is how accidents happen. Don't be a statistic.

- **View of the road:** Anticipate what's ahead: how does your closet serve you now? What kind of mileage has it had? Does it need to be refuelled? Will pimping your ride add value to your journey or will it just give you road rage?

Note: Meeting minimum acceptable standards does not ensure closet happiness for a further three years without regular maintenance, necessary for reliable and efficient operation. This is the sole duty of the closet's owner.

CURATING YOUR CLOSET: VISIBILITY IS ACCOUNTABILITY

Let's recap: you've found out what wayward emotions are driving your shopping habits. You've isolated and quarantined them. You've then got rid of everything from your closet that doesn't serve you and have filled in the blanks with a well-curated balance of trends and basics, keepsakes and happy purchases. Now what?

It's time for a spot of curating. Just like a gallery owner, your job is to select and present pieces that are individually resonant yet together tell a tale. So far, so good on the selecting. But what of the presentation?

It always amazes me how people pay top dollar for their clothes and yet feel short-changed when they die an untimely death. The lifespan of clothing can run the gamut from two washes and a prayer to coasting seamlessly across the generations. That said, the care that we administer to our wardrobe is fundamental to our closet happiness. There's nothing more dispiriting than seeing a perfectly lovely wool dress shrink to Barbie proportions on account of not reading the label. Likewise, if you're going to ball up a cashmere sweater into the back of your wardrobe, don't be too surprised to see a few holes and some hungover moths.

Remember: you're the curator of your own space – one that should reflect your more evolved and mindful self. If you owned a beautiful gallery, would you crowd the wall with every painting you thought might fit the brief? Of course not. There'd be no white space. And it's the white space – the pause, the ellipsis – that gives us a chance to breathe and appreciate what is right in front of us. Now that you've dispensed with old hang-ups and outdated habits, it's time to get us some proper hangers.

HANGERS: THE TOOLS OF THE TRADE

I am a stickler for hangers. When tasked with decluttering any closet, my first order of business is a deep and meaningful digression on proper hanger usage. I bring my own stash for demonstration purposes and a wagging finger of shame (patent pending) should things get ugly. This might be seen as taking it a bit too seriously. I say you can never be too serious about hangers. Why? Hangers are to clothes what a frame is to a photograph. By correctly arranging what's inside, you won't miss out on the important things, like Aunt Martha's ear or Cousin Timmy's head. Used properly, these humble tools can carry out a few basic but critical functions:

- Creating a unified and aesthetically pleasing display
- Helping you see what you have more clearly
- Increasing the lifespan of your clothes
- Making getting dressed a whole lot easier

That might be a rather impressive CV, but it's worth noting that not all hangers are created equal. As anyone who's seen Joan Crawford's infamous and incendiary rant in *Mommie Dearest* will attest, there's a sliding scale of what constitutes good hanger etiquette, starting at the bottom of the barrel – wire hangers.

Wire Hangers

Wire hangers are the bona fide delinquents of decent storage. Aggressive and capable of doubling as DIY weapons, their list of closet felonies include:

- Leaving marks on and misshaping the shoulders of shirts, blouses, dresses and jackets
- Causing discolouration, mildew and mould damage when found in the company of plastic covers from dry cleaners
- The potential to snag and damage delicate fabric
- The potential to rust when in contact with damp
- The potential to leave permanent marks and unsightly wrinkles on trouser legs.

It's safe to say that they are not to be trusted. Should you spy these closet offenders anywhere near your clothes, have them disposed of immediately. Do likewise when collecting anything from the dry cleaners. No good can come of it. Period.

Wooden and Velvet Hangers

Wooden and velvet hangers, on the others hand, are upstanding citizens and contribute to the general well-being of the clothing community. Even so, a bit of friendly rivalry exists between the two.

Strong and eco-friendly, wood is the Bear Grylls of the hanger world, boasting a natural moisture wicking and a unique ability to mimic the body's silhouette, thus allowing garments to retain their original shape. Although incredibly resilient, wood's hulky demeanour limits its options with smaller wardrobes and, unsanded, wood has the potential to snag fabric. And the rumours about wood being a natural moth-repellent? Slightly exaggerated – but more on that later.

The slim convenience of velvet, on the other hand, makes up for wood's lack of refinement, especially when it comes to hanging more delicate garments like silky tops or blouses. Surprisingly versatile, velvet can be colour-coded according to season and often comes with its own accessories like hooks and clips. That said, velvet's petite frame means it can lead to sharp creases and is known to break under too much pressure. It's also prone to a spot of dandruff.

There's no reason both can't peacefully co-exist. I personally use a combination of the two: wooden hangers for heavier items and delicate or expensive garments like suits and special dresses; and thinner velvet styles for easier, everyday pieces.

Specialty Hangers

It bears repeating that being precious about display brings

dividends. Like decent knickers, you might be the only one who sees them but there's no point shelling out shekels for a designer dress if you're sporting some questionable VPL. Ditto for hangers. Most good department and DIY stores stock specialty hangers for those pieces that deserve a little TLC. Some things are worth the extra attention.

Suit hangers: Protect and give added support to tailored jackets and trousers with their thick curved shape.

Contoured hangers: Ideal for jackets. Generally made from non-slip coated rubber. Thin but sturdy and take up less room than wood.

Padded hangers: Cushion the shoulder area on delicate knits, blouses and evening wear.

Clamp hangers: Great for storing skirts and pants (from the cuff) without leaving wrinkles or marks, and for strapless dresses.

Multi and tiered hangers: When space is at a premium, think vertically. These may be a fit for small spaces but their design can make garments a hassle to remove.

Accessory hangers: Great for belts, scarves and necklaces.

Sweater hangers: Their flocked shoulder flares help prevent knits sliding and stretching, although purists will argue that hanging is tantamount to sweater suicide.

Hookless hangers: Stuck for vertical space? No wardrobe in place? The Cliq hookless hanger from Flow Design attaches to any metallic tube or magnetic surface, giving extra room to those with very little.

How to Measure for a Hanger

- Using a measuring tape, measure the width of your shoulders from end to end. If you don't have someone to help you, then measure the fitted jacket you wear most often.
- The hangers you select should be approximately the same length – for example, 17.5 inches.
- According to TheSweetHome.com, the shoulder span on average hangers runs from 15 to 20 inches, so find one with no more than a 2–3-inch difference between the measurement of your own shoulders and the hanger.

HAPPINESS HACKS

- Never pull a hanger through the neck of a garment unless you want it to stretch like a Christmas turkey. The hem is always a safer bet.

- Floppy knee-high boots looking a bit sloppy? Hang boots by a skirt clamp on a separate rail.
- Weight matters. Opt for sturdier hangers (from 50 grams) to support heavier garments, especially coats and gowns.
- Protect leather pieces from unsightly marks by placing a piece of tissue paper or felt underneath hanger clips.
- Avoid plastic tubular hangers, which circle under your clothes, causing stretching and creasing of a garment at the shoulders.
- Top Keep or Cull tip: Using the swivel-head, face hangers in the same direction. Each time you wear a garment, simply reverse the direction of the hanger head. After six months, assess what hasn't been worn and decide whether to donate it or if it can be put to better use within the wardrobe.
- Hang trousers vertically from the waistline or cuff using a clamp hanger or folded by the crease to avoid leaving a line.
- Keep shirts ship-shape by buttoning the top-collar button and every second button after that – or, according to Martha Stewart, just the second button from the top.

HOW TO HANG AND FOLD THINGS: HAPPY CLOSET TECHNIQUES – GETTING THE HANG OF THINGS

Hanging clothes isn't exactly an art form but there's a certain knack to it. With a bit of know-how, combining order, space and colour is easily achievable, which is why I am rendered verklempt every time I witness a blouse suspended by the neck from a gallows, trousers dangling perilously from a wooden gibbet or jackets suffocating one on top of the other. If clothes could speak, there'd be some serious accusations doing the rounds, not to mention a whopper of a therapist's bill. Lest we raise a generation of damaged goods with a host of abandonment issues, this might be the best time to address our roles as closet caretakers. Let's start at the top.

Finding Order

The key to finding order is making life easy for yourself. Really easy. Basically, anything worn on a daily to weekly basis should go nearest the middle of a wardobe at eye level for speed and ease of use. Those items worn less frequently (occasion wear, special pieces) along with heavier items can go towards the edges. Easy.

Maintaining order takes a touch more finesse. Think of your wardrobe as a boutique and organise accordingly. Group garments according to type (jackets with jackets, trousers with trousers and so on), silhouette (blazers with blazers, skinny leg with skinny leg) and, finally, colour. Following this format is the simplest and most stress-free way to get dressed. Here's why:

- Sorting according to garment type and silhouette helps determine what you need and don't need. So you've got 23 blazers and no winter coat. Is that a default I smell?
- Sorting according to colour helps visualise an outfit as

separates and will lead you to mix and match combinations you may not have considered.

• Graduating hem lengths from long to short will create extra space on one side – ideal for creating extra room in smaller spaces.

The real yardstick of a happy closet is not having to think too hard. Six a.m. alarms, 'late again' dinner dashes and life waving its magic wand don't always allow for elongated musings over the unusual pairing of mustard and peacock blue. Sometimes it's a case of reach and run with barely enough time to hustle that zipper before calling a taxi. In times such as these, knowing the lie of the land makes life happier – infinitely so. Save the mustard–peacock blue debate for dinner convo.

Finally, assess the space between each garment. Clothes need room to breathe; otherwise, things will start to get a bit musty in there. Ensure there's enough leverage for removing and replacing pieces without causing a mosh-pit on the floor. Remember: extra space contributes to flow and general closet well-being. Nothing ever thrived in cramped conditions.

Folding Techniques

Everyone's got their own folding techniques: geometric precision, the military ranger roll, mother knows best and the less lauded but most common love 'em and leave 'em style. There's even a gravity-based robotic algorithm that's been developed by scientists at the University of California, Berkeley for the perfect fold, not to mention a YouTube-worthy Japanese origami technique made popular by high-street chain Uniqlo. All of these have a place in the tidying sphere, but if you're going to save space and therefore time, here are a few quick and dirty guidelines to help:

- Folding should protect the lifespan of the garment.
- Folding should allow you to see what you have at a glance.
- Folding should enhance the lifespan of your clothing while suiting your space needs.
- Folding should make your life easier.

As we now know, too much choice claps out willpower, which means unless you fancy sitting dazed and confused amid a pile of cardigans and crew-necks, it's best we break folding down to the most basic best practice.

Tops and T-Shirts

Question: What happens when you pull a T-shirt from the middle of a shop display?

Answer: A full-on cotton catastrophe complete with a mudslide of dirty looks from the underpaid sales assistant who just spent the past half hour folding them.

Not only are flat folded piles of tops tricky to keep tidy, they also take up a lot of space. The easiest way to avoid a clothing avalanche in your own closet is to go one extra step with your folding technique and stack like a filing cabinet. Either get your hands on a FlipFold folding board (available online and in most DIY stores) or go manual with the following steps:

- Place the top or T-shirt on a flat surface.
- From the shoulder seam, fold the garment on each side until it touches in the middle.
- From the hem, fold the garment to the middle and then fold once more to the back of the neck.
- Flip over and smooth.

Sweaters

Never hanging sweaters is up there with never lying and never wearing make-up to bed. We know we shouldn't but sometimes we just do because it's the easier option. There is one exception: those uber-fine knits that can use a sweater hanger, without being stretched like the political truth. There is a handy technique that allows for sweaters to be folded over a hanger, but a bulky rail just doesn't say 'happy closet'. Besides, folding comes with its own in-built insurance policy (unless it's cashmere – then special rules apply. See Chapter 10 for more). In the meantime, grab a shelf-divider or a dresser drawer and some tissue paper.

- Place the sweater on a flat surface.
- From the shoulder seam, fold the garment on each side until it touches in the middle.
- Place a piece of tissue paper on the sweater and from the

hem, fold the garment to the back of the neck, flip over and smooth. This will protect the garment from wrinkles and creases.

- To fold in thirds, fold once to the middle of the garment and again to the neck.
- Stack vertically in a dresser drawer or horizontally on a wardrobe shelf using a divider for extra neatness.

Jeans

Jeans are remarkably undemanding and don't need any special treatment per se – just a shelf. Give each pair its own hanger, however, and they'll take over the joint. Here's how to keep them in check:

- Lay jeans on a flat surface.
- Fold in half and smooth, pulling from the crotch to avoid bumps.
- Fold the bottom of the legs up to the yoke seam.
- Fold again, turn over, smooth and stack.

Underwear

There are generally two camps when it comes to smalls: those that go all-out Agent Provocateur style and those who rock a more utility vibe – nude multi-way bras and basic five-pack knickers. In my experience, those who indulge in lingerie show a bit more love than the 'grand, sure it'll do' brigade. (For the record, I fall squarely in the latter category. Standing accused.)

My point is that when we spend a bit of dosh on something, we're bound to look after it and treat it with a bit more care. It's the disposability theory at play again. Now, one may argue that underwear has a lot more to deal with than simply looking sexy or making one feel a bit frisky. True. But a mix of functionality and frippery never did anyone any harm. Having a collection of expensive knickers is a bit like being made to stand next to the best-dressed person in the room. Suddenly you feel like you need to make more of an effort.

- Lay your smalls out on a flat surface with the front side facing up and one end of the waistband towards you.
- Fold the crotch up. It should be even with the top of the underwear.
- Fold each side of the waistband inward, allowing the ends to meet in the centre.
- Flip the underwear over so that it is shaped like a square.
- Stack them vertically inside your drawers by colour.

Failing that, you can always lay them flat and roll them tightly from one side until they form a de facto knicker Swiss roll. Then stack them side-by-side for easy access.

When it comes to our bras, a bit less engineering is required. Simply stand them upright – one in front of the other, colour by colour – until they form a type of brassiere library. Last season's Bali balconette? You'll find that three bras over in the rose-pink section. You see? Easy.

Socks

Marie Kondo, author of *The Life-Changing Magic of Tidying*, has big respect for socks. I take her point. Like your underwear, socks need a bit of love. They cover your feet, get shoved into shoes and are subject to sharp nails and rips. They've really drawn the short end of the stick. Go easy on them. Instead of pairing and rolling them into an inside-out sock doughnut, try this gentler method.

· Take one pair of socks and tuck the toes together.

· Fold the elastic side over, making thirds of the sock.

· Open the elastic of the folded side.

· Then tuck the toes of both socks in the elastic.

· It should resemble a rectangle, which lends itself to stacking and easier access.

Store or Display?

This is where it gets interesting. Anything that doesn't receive the hanger treatment is generally that which needs most attention. Take a quick gawk into your wardrobe and you might find some tangled scarves, shoes still in their boxes, necklaces entwined together – you get the picture. In order to be accountable for our closet collateral, *everything* needs to be visible. This is especially good for Secret Shoppers who thrive on stashing their swag in cubby holes and impenetrable corners. Nowhere to hide now, my friend!

Shoes

Lining up your footwear at the bottom of a closet heel-to-toe may be the most obvious solution for storing one's tootsie rolls but it's also a dusty and potentially messy one. Any time you hang up a long coat or dress – *swoosh* – there goes a shoe. Unless you've got a bespoke display unit in your closet (one of my clients converted a bookshelf for her shoe collection), take some inspiration from the suggestions below. Just remember to always keep shoes away from direct sunlight and to ensure there's enough breathing space between each pair.

- Shoe racks make life easier, as do wall upright shoe organisers or mounted picture rails that are both space-saving and do decorative double-duty.

- Tension rods also help maximise redundant closet space. Simply hang shoes by the heel.

- Shelving units make handy display cases (store toe-to-heel for extra space) as do clear stackable storage bins.

- Invest in shoe- and boot-trees. While it's always better to keep your boots standing upright, if space is at a premium, lay them flat on their sides (make sure to condition them first) in clear plastic bins covered in a pillow case or muslin shoe-bag.

- Afraid to expose your Miu Mius to the elements? Keep designer shoes in a box with the shoe picture facing forward.

Bags

In some cultures, leaving a bag on the floor is considered bad luck as doing so symbolically demonstrates our attitude to money, which is generally nestled in our purses. Yet it never ceases to amaze me how many totes, clutches, backpacks and holdalls I see stashed and forsaken at the bottom of a wardrobe. It's the equivalent of tempting fate, and fate, as far as I'm concerned, is worthy of the good biscuits and the fancy china cups – not wanton neglect. The solution?

- Letter-holders and magazine racks make ideal dividers for the fiddly, floppy, teensy or unstructured.
- Hang bags from S-hooks on an extra closet rail (or tension rod). Hardcore bag ladies may disagree with that method lest it stretches the handles, but I've hung clutches from the zip that way and smaller bags from their handles in the same way without incurring damage.
- If this still unnerves you, then store bags in cubby hole dividers or a multiple display unit inserted into bare corners, nailed to a wall or placed atop a free-standing clothing rail.
- Always remember to keep arm candy out of direct sunlight. If in doubt, place it in its dust bag.

Scarves, Jewellery, Belts & Bits

Belts are a horror to hang. Give them a hook and they'll either fall off at the slightest provocation or get tangled up in the adjacent belt just hanging out minding its own business. They're scrappy like that. Although specialist hangers exist, my feeling is why pander to them? I'd rather put the little beggars in their place, rolled up tightly and stored in individual pockets of a dresser drawer organiser where they belong. Alternatively, bung them into a wire basket where they can be seen and not heard.

Scarves can be rolled or folded like socks, stored bra-filing-cabinet style or given their own space with drawer dividers. For those partial to a bit of Hermès or other purveyors of silk squares, try a specialist scarf hanger and drape accordingly.

Jewellery isn't without its complications. Although a velvet display unit dispenses with the fussiness of individual boxes, sometimes special and more expensive pieces need particular care and attention. Cheaper costume baubles can hang out in anything from an armoire to china cups or, in the case of bangle, a mug tree. The sky's the limit. As for the snazzy stuff, whether gold or silver, gemstones, diamonds or pearls, the following always applies:

- Avoid tarnishing by keeping away from moisture, direct sunlight and heat.
- Avoid scratching by storing each piece separately in individual breathable fabric bags.
- Store diamonds in a fabric-lined box or divider case.
- Keep a tarnish-proof cloth to hand for buffing silver.
- Store pearl necklaces flat to avoid stretching and keep away from very dry conditions which can cause small surface fractures.

Off-Season: Non-Seasonal & Sentimental Pieces

If you happen to live in a temperate climate, chances are you've got a unified closet front nailed. If, like many of us, precocious weather patterns dictate much of what you wear from season to season, then spare storage space is expected, if not encouraged. There's no reason to keep a Polar Express down-quilted full-length hooded coat to hand when the sun is splitting the rocks. Nor do diaphanous maxi-dresses really warrant hanger space when horizontal hailstones are offering hourly frosty facials (free of charge!). Once the leaves turn or the mercury starts to rise, finding a place to store your off-season goodies that is neither too hot nor too cold, neither too dusty nor too damp becomes a pressing question. Shopping-channel vacuum-pack storage bags may seem like a boon for the space-deprived (or the lazy) but shrink-wrapping your favourite threads comes at a hefty price – namely, damage. If you plan on maintaining the happiness of your closet year on year, getting familiar with storage etiquette is key. And entertaining an attic or a basement for storing anything sentimental or expensive is simply asking for it. Here's why.

Location, Location, Location

Attics are hard to seal, sensitive to temperature fluctuations and a happy hunting ground for dust, mites and insects like silverfish, carpet beetles and moths that would love nothing more than to nibble at your favourite Norse sweater or silk shirtdress. Natural fibres are their weakness. Basements, garages, garden sheds – anything that attracts damp – is also a potential disaster. Basically, unless you have a small wardrobe or a cool, dry storage area in your living quarters that can be used (strictly!) for off-season and sentimental pieces, the best bet is to depend on furnishings that can do double-duty, such as vintage suitcases and decorative trunks. Or you could take the Swedish space-saving approach and decorate unused shelves with storage baskets, crates and wicker boxes. Websites like Apartment Therapy (ApartmentTherapy.com) and the doyenne of all things domestic Martha Stewart (MarthaStewart. com) are genius resources whether you are living in a studio flat with no cat to swing or a four-bed semi in the suburbs. For even more visual inspiration, come visit my Pinterest page (at www. thehappycloset.me) where I've also cherry-picked some of the more novel closet happiness tips.

Keep It Clean

Wash everything before storing it away. EVERYTHING. Why? Imperceptible oil stains (fingers, moisturiser) can oxidise and leave permanent marks. Worse still, insects (especially the female adult moth) are attracted to food and perspiration stains, not to mention starch and fabric softener. Do your threads a favour and opt for a detergent-only lullaby before putting them to bed for the season.

A Word about Wood

Wood has been receiving possibly a bit too much glory time in hanger circles. Cedar, the kingpin of wooden hangers, is often touted as a natural moth repellent but cedar itself does not kill insects. It's the aroma of the oils in cedar that's highly irritating to insects and makes them less likely to stay in that vicinity for a prolonged period of time. But in order for cedar to be aromatic, it has to be unfinished. Sanding the wood will help bring up the aroma, as will applying a coat of cedar oil, but that still doesn't solve the bigger issue. Wood is highly acidic and releases acid with age. When acids get physical with your garments, they do so with some iffy consequences – namely, by causing them to yellow and deteriorate. Handy happiness hack? Line the inside of any chest of drawers or shelves with a chemically inert barrier sheet like polyester felt or pH-neutral tissue.

Cover It Up

OK. So we know that clothes should be stored somewhere cool and dry and in an acid-free environment. This means you should use:

- A cotton-canvas bag if hanging, or a cotton pillow case or bedsheet if you go DIY-style (just add a hole for the hanger head)
- A cloth or acid-free archival box if folding.

And never use:

- Nylon or vinyl garment bags
- Vacuum-pack storage bags
- Plastic boxes or plastic bags, including those from the dry cleaner
- Cotton or canvas zip-up suit bags with clear plastic fronts
- Anything cedar.

And never store:

- In an attic
- In a basement
- Anywhere dusty.

Start with heavy items first like coats and jackets. Button up, remove any random items from pockets, fold and stack loosely to encourage air flow and discourage mildew. Try and keep like with like where possible (jeans with jeans, sweaters with sweaters) and don't be tempted to roll and shove thinner tops down the sides of boxes. This will only make your clothes look like they've spent a season on the Underground at rush hour – creased, damp and slightly malodorous. Delicate fabrics like silk, organza, tulle and cashmere need to be wrapped in acid-free tissue paper and placed in a cotton-canvas bag. If cashmere is your thing, skip to Chapter 10 for special instructions on how to care for its finicky fibres. Speaking of which, anything fur has its own celebrity rider – ideally, its own climate-controlled space at 7–10°C and approximately 50% humidity. Living in a hot climate? Don't risk it. Get grandma's mink stored in a professional vault. Finally, any shoes or boots should be wiped down, packed with tissue paper to maintain their shape and stored in their dust-bags. Finally, don't forget to throw in some lavender or rosemary sachets to keep any winged visitors away.

STORAGE CHEATSHEET

Blinded by science? Here's the abridged version.

DISPLAY

- T-shirt folder
- Shoe rack or shoe boxes
- Wall upright shoe organiser
- Picture rail
- Tension rod
- Shoe tree
- Magazine racks or letter-holders
- S-hooks
- Free-standing clothing rail
- Adjustable drawer dividers
- Baskets, crates or wicker boxes

HANGERS

- Wood
- Velvet
- Suit
- Contoured
- Padded
- Clamp
- Multi and tiered
- Accessory
- Sweater
- Hookless

STORAGE

- T-shirts, jeans: clear plastic boxes
- Anything delicate or valuable: acid-free boxes
- Spare cotton pillowcases and sheets
- Cotton-canvas storage bags/clothes cover
- Wooden or cloth boxes with lids
- Acid-free paper
- Tissue paper
- Rosemary or lavender sachets

INSIDE A STYLIST'S KIT BAG: TREATMENT – KEEPING THE LIFE IN WHAT YOU LOVE

Being a stylist is a bit like being MacGyver. Often you're required to save a dress from falling apart with just a stick of gum and a two-inch piece of wire or save a four-figure suede jacket from sudden demise with sandpaper or a stale crust of bread. These are skills they never teach you in school but that prove their worth when it comes to looking put-together – and staying put-together. Conveniently, these kit-bag items multi-task in a variety of ways that make them both ordinary heroes and veritable life-savers. In the interests of closet happiness, I'd suggest you grab an empty bag and fill 'er up accordingly. You never know what emergency might require a spare heel-cap and a bra extender.

Measuring tape: They call them vital statistics for a reason; plus, it's also fun to measure the circumference of your head.

Vaseline: Slicks brows into place, removes intransigent rings, helps swollen feet slide into tight shoes.

Safety pins: Buttons pop, fabric rips and seams fall apart like a bad reality show script. You need these guys on your team.

Bondaweb: Rescues hems with the help of a hair straightener or iron.

Vanish pen: Removes stains on the go.

Button adjusters: Kiss fat days goodbye with these handy waistline expanders.

Boob tape: Because the girls can get rowdy.

Chicken fillets: Insta-boob – need I say more?

Masking tape: For covering shoe soles for shoots and shows. Handy if you run out of boob tape.

Silk scarf: For putting over your face when trying on clothes to prevent make-up stains.

Underarm pads: For Sweaty Betties.

Bra strap clips and extender: For tricky dress styles.

Shoe horn: The polite way to slide feet into shoes.

Gel soles: Rescues feet from unavoidably long nights in heels.

Lint brush: Key to not looking lived-in and love-worn.

Bobble-off: Because no one ever said 'nice bobbles' and meant your sweater.

Sewing kit: From needles to spools of threads and mini-scissors.

Insoles: Stop feet smelling, prevent calf strain and save knees.

Shoe-shine kit: The shampoo, conditioner and blow-dry of footwear.

Water spritz bottle: To help steam out creases.

Shaving cream: Removes stains from white leather and make-up stains from collars.

Nipple covers: To avoid any de facto weather reports.

Nude thongs: To prevent see-through moments under white clothing.

Nail file: Because rough nail edges rip tights, snag delicate fibres and generally cause havoc.

Hairspray: Stops tights laddering – just spray before wearing.

Static guard: Clingy is not a good look.

Deodorant remover: No good ever came of a damp patch.

Spare heel-caps: Cobbles, uneven pavement and steel-gridded stairs live to destroy stilettos.

Talcum powder: Removes oil stains.

Mini hair straightener: To iron collars and cuffs.

Moisturiser: Removes scratches from leather.

Garment brush: For quickly removing fluff, bits and general airborne detritus.

Lavender sachets: Moth-repellent because nothing says 'die clothes, die!' like a hungry winged creature.

Hand steamer: The hassle-free way to remove wrinkles on the go; can help save on dry cleaning costs too.

Small bottle of window cleaner: Shines up patent shoes.

Crust of stale bread: Cleans dirt from suede (no, I don't carry this around but it's a good tip nonetheless!).

PUTTING THE APP IN HAPPY – TECHNOLOGY

Ah, the hydra-headed beast that is technology! What we gain in time and productivity, we lose in – *time and productivity*. And money. Let's not forget the money. Fancy a glass or three of vino on a Friday night? Step away from the laptop, lady! Maybe Google Labs could invent an add-on whereby a series of maths questions must be answered before being allowed access to eBay. 'What is your current credit card balance?' would do nicely or 'How many months would it take to pay off that Gucci jumpsuit at a 9.5% APR?' I prefer the idea of a real-time Skype intervention with your bank manager each time that 'purchase' button is pressed. Much scarier. As with most things in the digital age, there's an app for that. Not the scary bank manager one (not yet, anyway) but some rather effective tools to help keep your closet and habits in check.

Stylebook

What it promises: Stylebook is designed to help you carefully curate your wardrobe and take the stress out of getting dressed.

What it offers: Over 90 features, from a cost-per-wear calculator to style stats, that provide an overview of your highest performing and most under-utilised pieces.

How it helps: Its various features help you monitor and update your wardrobe, ensuring you buy pieces that count. The added shock value of seeing how much you've spent on clothes can be a boon to impulse buyers and those looking to shop more mindfully.

How it hinders: Photographing and archiving every item of clothing involves a considerable time investment, not to mention having to regularly update inventory whenever you cull from or add items to your closet. Not ideal for technophobes, the time-strapped or impatient.

Coach.me

What it promises: Helps form and sustain desired habits with a single-step approach to change.

What it offers: A user chooses habit(s) to cultivate and checks in whenever the intended action is performed. Accomplishing the intended action is your victory party and the app allows you to celebrate it with a Facebook-inspired act of check-in. 'Momentum' is used as a yardstick to measure how near you are to making the habit your habit. In order to gain 'Momentum' on the app, you need to perform and check in a habit at least three times a week.

How it helps: The users community acts as a buddy system (which is proved to help maintain good habits) that provides healthy peer pressure and encouragement through 'props' (likes) for your check-ins. Props, as a form of peer recognition, can fuel motivation. Users can also opt for paid one-to-ones with experts in the specific field they wish to master.

How it hinders: The regular notifications and reminders might not be compatible with those who juggle a varied daily schedule.

stickK

What it promises: Helps stop procrastination by getting you to pre-commit to a goal that must be completed by a certain deadline.

What it offers: Before you start the process, you have to pay a small fee. If you miss your deadline, the money becomes locked and is donated to a charity you hate.

How it helps: It galvanises users with passion, a sense of duty and integrity. It also works on the most pliable emotion of all

– guilt. Imagine how bad you'd feel if you thought you were responsible for funding the Charles Manson Appreciation Society?

How it hinders: There are other options that don't involve laying down any cash, which defeats the purpose of this unorthodox but seemingly effective brain scare method.

Balanced

Mindful time management.

What it promises: Tracks the things you wish you did most often and motivates you to do them again and again.

What it offers: Balanced is designed to create positive changes with mindful motivation and a focus on rewards. Select a life-affirming activity (declutter), an icon (hanger, anyone?) and decide how often (once a week, twice a month) it should be completed. Activities are intelligently ordered according to importance, with simple timelines, daily reminders, helpful nudges ('do soon', 'do now', 'what would bring you greater happiness today?') and comparison functions to keep you on track. See when you last did each task, when you're on a streak, and complete with a celebratory swipe. Balance will acknowledge your win ('You're obviously getting the hang of things!') and make you want to do the happy dance.

How it helps: Balance is like a Zen cheerleader who keeps you on the good path. The app is particularly helpful in building a competing response to a bad habit (painting instead of power shopping?) or simply re-engaging with a life-affirming one without the resentment of traditional task management.

How it hinders: It doesn't. Its sheer simplicity makes it a winner. (Note: A lot of the juicier features are only available with an upgrade, but they're worth the nominal fee.)

The Vane

What it promises: Integrates the forecast, destination and purpose of your trip with curated clothing suggestions (from product to street-style shots) to take the stress out of getting dressed for holidays.

What it offers: With the help of an algorithm that combines your personal details (age, personal style, temperament) with the weather forecast, The Vane can intuitively suggest suitable outfits by occasion, location and inspiration. Missing something from the list? Buy straight from the app.

How it helps: The most useful feature is 'Pack to Travel', which helps prep your suitcase for any destination with a checklist based on your travel dates, trip purpose (business or pleasure) and expected temperature. Got an outfit you love? Save a photo on the day it was worn and the app will recommend it again when similar weather does the rounds.

How it hinders: The social element of the app, although relevant in that it powers more user-specific outfit recommendations, can be more frivolous than functional when scrolling through selfies.

Vinted

What it promises: Helps facilitate the decluttering process with the dangling carrot of recouping some of the financial loss from unworn or gently worn items.

What it offers: Vinted offers a place to buy, sell or swap used or unwanted clothing. Place a photo of what you're selling online with a description and a price and wait for interested parties to barter for a suitable price or potential swap. Do business, send your swag and get paid when the item arrives safely to its new owner.

How it helps: If you don't live near a charity shop and eBay scares the bejesus out of you, then Vinted is for you. Buyers benefit from a nifty Pinterest-board style feed function which helps filter wish-list items according to sizes and brands.

CLEARING THE SPACE FOR CHANGE

How it hinders: As a vendor, you're in charge of hustling your wares with decent photos and keywords to stand out from the crowd. You also have to dispatch goods in a timely manner and sort postage and packaging. As a buyer, you're relying on the honesty of other vendors.

CH-CH-CH-CHANGES ...

So how is your closet beginning to look? Different? Fresher? Have you started to see yourself in the change? Exciting, isn't it? For now. You see, as much as we resist change, when we do experience it, we adapt to it just as easily. If not treated as an ongoing process, that well-curated closet of yours will soon acquire the sepia tinge of old memories. The once heady excitement will recede to a hazy familiarity and soon enough old habits will re-emerge. Excuses will subtly undermine effort and before you know it, the relationship that gave you goosebumps will leave you cold. How did it all happen? You don't even know. As covered in Chapter 6, keeping the love alive is really about keeping present – being consciously and continuously aware of your evolving needs. And what is mindfulness but another way of saying 'to pay close attention'? You see, a happy closet is more than just a physical space – it's a mindset, one that keeps the flow flowing and the go going. Adding the extra to your ordinary doesn't involve multiple costume changes, a wardrobe team and three truckloads of designer swag. Quite the opposite. It's a simple shift in perspective – is your closet half empty or half full? Let's see, shall we?

CHAPTER NINE

WELL-BEING IS WELL-DRESSED

REFLECTIONS

'The secret of happiness, you see, is not found in seeking more, but in developing the capacity to enjoy less.'

SOCRATES

'Simplicity is the ultimate sophistication.'

LEONARDO DA VINCI

Remember when I first asked you how you felt when you opened your closet? Let's revisit that question. How do you feel *now* when you open your closet? That sense of dread and insecurity should have dissipated to a soufflé-like levity, a sense of calm and unfettered ease – well-being if you will. That's the beauty of reflection – we see our new selves mirrored back in the pool of what we once were. And look how far you've come.

Now that we've distanced the Impulse from the Buyer and the Sniper from the Sale, woken up the Tired and soothed the Emotional, helped Black Widows and Split Personalities heal, kept Secret Shoppers accountable and Doomsday Preppers present, all the while preserving Perfect 9s from Rutsville and getting Martyr Moms out of theirs, I do believe a toast is in order – or perhaps even a little victory dance.

Before we get the party started, we've got one order of business left. In order to maintain this newfound mojo, it helps to have a set of guidelines to keep us on the good path lest we get so consumed with our shiny new image that we forget who we really are. Consider it your Closet Happiness Credo – a summation of sartorial wellness in ten truths. Simple truths. Nothing fancy. No shopping-channel sales pitch – while stocks last, order now pay later, 30-day free trial, recommend a friend, cancel if you're not happy (but not before we get your credit card details); no downloadable code, free gift, swanky wrapping paper or revolutionary promise. Why? Because sometimes simplicity is its own reward.

THE TEN TRUTHS OF CLOSET HAPPINESS

1. Let the outside reflect the inside

How do your Core Closet Values align with your lifestyle? This is something you should ask yourself every year. Treat your clothing collection as a government tasked with ministering to your needs. Does it serve the greater good? How does it contribute to the Gross National Happiness of your closet? (Bhutan measures abundance by gauging the happiness levels of its citizens.) Are there any garments that need to be re-elected or should you tender their resignation? You get to decide who stays and who goes.

2. Learn from the past – just don't take it with you

There's a lesson in everything – even that toga dress with the voluminous draping that made you look like you were concealing weapons across border control. I know, I know. It was a great idea at the time but that time has passed. Best leave the Greco-Roman homage to frat boys, Halloween parties and die-hard neoclassists.

3. Accept who you are now but watch who you become

So, you've still got stretch marks from that beautiful baby you miraculously created or maybe you're living in a tiny flat-share with three others while saving for your own place. Circumstances are malleable and life sometimes leaves scars. Moreover, identity isn't a fixed attribute. There's always room for change but while you're jonesing for tomorrow, don't forget to respect that person in the mirror and dress her like a bad-ass – she deserves it.

4. Get to know yourself and your image through the eyes of others

What we don't know about ourselves could fill volumes. Sometimes all it takes is an outside perspective to give us real clarity. Just make sure the truth-givers are worthy of the title. Everything else is just an opinion.

5. Face up to procrastination

The only time you should be putting off anything is on a golf course; otherwise you're only delaying the inevitable. Are you dangling from a bungee rope that is slowly slipping off your ankles? No? Swimming in shark-infested waters with a bag of week-old chum strapped to your body? No, I didn't think so. The prospect of facing your fears is often greater than the sum of all fears – unless you *are* slipping from a bungee over shark-infested waters with a bag of week-old chum strapped to your bag. Then you're allowed to panic.

6. Allow for space – don't fill it

Have you ever stood on an empty beach overlooking a vast expanse of ocean? All that's between you and the end of the earth is gravity and space. So calm, so energising. Now imagine a crowded beach filled with litter, loud music, ice-cream hawkers and more people than one stretch of sand could possibly accommodate without risking health and safety. Now ask yourself, why would you want to fill your beautiful wardrobe?

7. Put limitations on choice

Don't mistake clutter for abundance. It shouldn't take a hybrid algorithm and a Venn diagram to get dressed. The more limitations we put on choice, the less confusion, the less stress and the more our creativity can flourish. Possibilities expand as life slows down – not the other way around. By choosing deliberately and mindfully, we begin to understand the *why* behind our clothing and, in turn, find more purpose, direction and meaning. Think of it as a small business versus a large corporation – smaller businesses tend to have fewer resources but bigger hearts and far less anonymity. Pare things back and get on first-name terms with what you wear. You won't regret it.

8. Create a signature

Those with a strong sense of self have well-defined boundaries. Ditto those with a strong sense of style. The secret? Creating a look from limited options – one that is immediately identifiable as yours. Align these choices with what you truly value – whether it's a life-long love of lilac or the cognitive ease of a jumpsuit – and feel their liberating effects, in terms of both time and mental space.

9. Harness the three Hs

There is zilcho point in decluttering your closet unless you've first decluttered your mind. You know the drill: it's the *Hang-ups* driving our *Habits* that shape our long-term closet *Happiness*. Get to grips with the unresolved emotional issues behind your shopping behaviour if you are serious about achieving closet harmony. Ignore them and you'll be doomed to repeat the past – again and again and again.

10. Upgrade your relationship

It's time to get serious. No more flings, no more one-night stands, no more walks of shame. If you want true commitment from your clothing, you'd best be prepared to put in the graft. Don't rely on slick advertisements and external endorsements to find the one. The real deal takes honesty, vulnerability and a whole lot of moxie. Only true love has the power to go the distance. How far are you willing to go?

Time's up, folks. This is officially where our session ends and I take my leave. It's over to you now. Allow me, though, to leave you with one thought: closet happiness doesn't require a footwear collection to rival that of the Bata shoe museum, nor does it demand the sycophantic attention of a celebrity-style rider. It's the sweet spot that exists between you and your clothing – the feeling you get from wearing what you love and loving what you wear.

You've done all the heavy lifting, so now it's time to raise a glass. Here's to derailing your hang-ups and giving bad habits the bum's rush. Here's to confronting your inner hoarder, your inner coward and your inner critic. Here's to isolating rogue impulses, mastering the retail jungle and purging the urge to splurge. Here's to setting fire to that security blanket and learning how to let go. Here's to punching procrastination in the goolies and becoming the doyenne of decluttering. Here's to figuring out what makes you tick. Most of all, here's to you. Welcome to your happy closet – this is your space, so fill it wisely.

Your closet therapist,

Annmarie x

CHAPTER TEN

HAPPY CLOSET HOW-TOS

HOW TO MEASURE YOURSELF

'It's not denial. I'm just selective about the reality I accept.'

BILL WATTERSON

Denial:

noun: a mythical place where Bollinger runs in rivers, everyone is a size 8 and cellulite an urban myth. Often accompanied by 'magic mirrors' and 'vanity sizing'.

Confession time. I remember being measured (not so long ago) by a seamstress. 'I'm a 36‑27–36,' I pre-empted. 'You're a 36–29–38,' she replied. Refusing to engage with such inflated numbers, I demanded a recount. Clearly I was not the first woman to remonstrate; she asked me to show her how I measure myself. Believing the extra two abdominal inches were due to some recent carb-loading (and not indicative of my actual size), I skipped straight to my hip bones. 'You see, that's where you're going wrong,' she chided gently. 'You're about two inches off the mark.' And with that she let the cold hard tape of truth slide over the top of my thighs resting comfortably on the ease of my bottom. The evidence was irrefutable. And there I believed Heidi Klum and I could swap clothes.

It's not that I'm totally clueless. My mother, a dressmaker, made many of my childhood frocks from Vogue and Butterick patterns. Aged 13, I crafted my first jersey Breton shift in Sr Eithne's Home Economics class; and now, as a fully grown stylist, I'm rarely without a measuring tape on my person. Shame on me.

Call it wishful thinking or inductive reasoning, but my outright denial of the facts (until third-party intervention) was admittedly the reason behind a lot of my past dressing decisions. That bit too tight, a smidgen too short, could do with an extra inch of breathing space – I would search, interpret and prioritise information to confirm my own size 10 hypothesis. Well, slap my thigh and call me vain but I could have done with that reality check a bit earlier. The fact is, emotionally charged issues (weight being the top bugbear for most women) make the denial effect all the stronger.

With that, it's absolutely vital to get to grips with your true vital statistics – a life skill that should be taught along with changing tyres, networking and opening a bottle of wine without a corkscrew. File this one under 'useful life hacks'.

Vital Statistics – A User's Guide

Basics: Using a soft tape, stand straight in front of a full-length mirror and read the measurement directly from the mirror as opposed to looking down.

Bust: Place one end of the tape measure at the widest part of your bust (while wearing a bra), make sure it wraps under your armpits and around your shoulder blades and back to get the measurement.

Under-bust: Wrap the tape under your bust, where the bra band would sit, to get your under-bust measurement.

Bra size: Round up your bust size to the nearest measurement. Subtract your under-bust size from the rounded-up number. Add approximately one cup size for every inch difference. A difference of one leaves you with an A cup, while a difference of two equals a B cup, three equals a C cup and four equals a D cup.

Waist: Measure the circumference of your waist. Use the tape to circle your waist at your natural waistline (above your belly button and below your rib cage). Keep the tape parallel to the floor and don't be tempted to suck in your stomach or you'll get a false measurement.

Hips: Wrap the tape measure around the fullest part of your hips and bum. This is about seven to nine inches below your natural waist. Keep the tape measure parallel to the floor and don't cheat by pulling too tightly on the band.

Upper arms and thighs: Measure around the widest part of your upper arm and thigh.

Inseam: This is the distance from the uppermost inner part of your thigh to the bottom of your ankle. Tip: If buying trousers to be worn with heels, add the heel heights to your inseam measurement.

Sleeve length: Recruit a friend for this one. With your hand on your waist and elbow bent at a 90-degree angle, measure from the middle of the back of your neck to your shoulder, down your arm to the elbow, and then on to the wrist.

Gloves: Wrap a measuring tape around your dominant hand (the one you use most) below the knuckles (and minus the thumb) for width. For finger length, measure from the tip of your middle finger to the bottom edge of your palm.

Hats: Gently wrap the tape around the circumference of the head above the ears, making sure it lies across the bump in the middle of the back of your head. Measure a few times for accuracy and don't pull too tightly.

See how you measure up by logging onto www.thehappycloset.me for international sizing charts.

HOW TO PUT ON A BRA

'Stoop, *then* scoop!' My sister leaned forward and made digging motions at her bra as if working at some sort of boob gelateria. She seemed keen to impart what appeared to be common knowledge – just not so common with me. 'And you wonder why yours are so flat,' she said, raising her scooping hands despairingly in the air. It's true, though. I always did wonder why, despite sharing the same bra size, her assets always looked perkier than mine. It just never occurred to me that scooping could play a factor.

Maybe that's because at the age of 12, I harassed my mother for a training bra when my new recruits hadn't even turned up to camp. So the whole how-to-put-on-a-bra tutorial was effectively a moot point. I'd clasp it at the front, reef it around my back, strap it over my shoulders and go about my merry size AA way. I knew the basic mechanics of loosening when too tight and tightening when too loose but invariably I'd always be left with the battle scars of restricted blood supply or the tell-tale marks of muffin back or boob overspill. What's more, I didn't have a rasher about how adjusting your breast tissue could create twin peaks as opposed to my obvious troughs. Who knew? Slightly more enlightened, I'm here to share with you some uplifting advice.

Clasping: Elementary as it may sound, there's a knack to getting your girls into place. Whether you're dexterous enough to adjust from the back or, like me, need to clasp from the front, you should use the middle set of hooks first and, as the band gets looser with wear, adjust to the inside clasp.

Strapping: Ensure the straps fit properly over your shoulders. Too tight? Is it digging into your skin? Any unsightly back fat or armpit overspill? Look in the mirror: does the back band sit higher than the cups? Time to lower those straps so that they sit evenly.

Stooping: Stand up and lean forward. Jiggle your bra to make sure your breasts are sitting in your cups with the nipple centred forward.

Scooping: Taking two fingers, scoop from the side under the armpit up towards the centre. This will eliminate any rogue skin bulges along the way.

Smoothing: Finally, run your index finger along the inside front edges of your bra cup to smooth out any lumps.

Think of it like putting the kids to bed each night: cover them up, adjust and tuck 'em in.

HOW TO WALK IN HEELS

I grew eight inches, almost overnight, when I was 13. Not dissimilar to a baby giraffe, I had a spot of bother in the walking-straight department. My newly extended limbs flapped, flailed and floundered, which was fun for a time – until they got tangled in one another and I invariably fell flat on my face. A bit like Dusty Springfield, I just didn't know what to do with myself. My mother sought to remedy this situation before the next growing spurt and, more important, before anyone lost an eye.

I was given a pair of two-inch almond-toe courts for my then size 7 feet and a stack of books for my head. The challenge? To successfully traverse the hallway in heels without the collected works of Jane Austen crashing to its demise. Suffice to say, *Pride and Prejudice* was a bit dented and *Emma* looked somewhat scuffed but after a few turns on the polished tiles (because *that* really helped – thanks, Mom), the old-fashioned lesson in poise stood me in good stead.

To this day, I neither shuffle nor do I plod. Granted, I don't stomp like Giselle but, in fairness, I don't think the *Victoria's Secret* show was my mother's end-game. The result? I'm unapologetically 6 foot tall and even taller in heels. I own my height, not the other way around. Regardless of how tall or short you may be, there'll always a time when you'll need or want to wear heels. A dress hem may require it, you may wish to elongate your legs or damn it, you may just want to sway your hips like a metronome on a Friday night. In any case, here are a few pointers. And if none of these stick, grab some books and start walking.

Make sure your heels fit: Too big? Add in a heel grip. Too small? Don't wear them unless your idea of sexy is a foot full of bunions.

Slow it down: You know how quickly you walk in those Nike Air Max trainers? Halve that, then halve it again. Heels are not made for speed; they're made for slower strides.

Lean back: The architecture of a heel is such that it throws the body forward ever so slightly. The result? You wind up craning your neck like a curious zoo creature. Not the desired effect? Gently press the knuckle of your forefinger at the base of your spine and – bingo – posture! Trust me, this works – my mom used to do it.

Take smaller steps: You've officially strapped a four-inch spike to your heels and now you want to run for that bus? Nooooooo. Smaller steps decrease your chances of a face-to-pavement collision and, while you're at it, take a taxi.

Walk heel-to-toe: Get into the habit of walking heel-to-toe and watch how your body leans back and your stride starts to soften. Instant grace.

Relax: Resist the urge to tense up your knees and hips. Not only does this make you look rigid when walking, you're more likely to resemble a chalk outline after a bad accident. The idea is to stay upright at all times.

HOW TO PUT ON TIGHTS

In life there are some inconvenient truths: everything will break at the same time, someone will steal your parking space and a lack of toilet paper will only be noticed when your arse is planted firmly on the throne. Sh*t happens. So do ripped tights. Regardless of whether you bought those 15-denier beauties from a vending machine or the Triangle d'Or, they will fast resemble Courtney Love after a night on the razz if you don't follow these four simple steps.

Step 1: Slap
Moisturise those gams. Slap on and rub in a thick lotion over fuzz-free legs (wax or shave, take your pick). Dry skin is the enemy of hosiery – especially that which is especially sheer. While you're at it, file those toenails lest a rogue digit vex the delicate fabric.

Step 2: Slip

Remove jewellery and slip on a pair of gloves to avoid fingernail snags. Any ones will do (aside from the ski or mitten variety) but the thinner the better – nick your kid's communion gloves or buy latex ones from the pharmacy. Just keep those talons under cover.

Step 3: Stretch

Some tights are a bit mean – no give, none at all. If yours are somewhat parsimonious, gently pull from top to toe and side to side before putting them on to avoid any instances of mid-thigh gridlock. Most annoying.

Step 4: Slide

Holding the waist, gingerly bunch one leg from waist to toe with both thumbs until it resembles a closed accordion or a condom – take your visual pick. Curl your toes to avoid popping the tip of the tights and pull the tight gently over the length of the leg, taking care not to rip or snag along the way. Alternate with the other leg. If dealing with troublesome tights, simply roll back down and start again.

Step 5: Smooth

Extend your leg and smooth the tights from heel to thigh, making sure to even out any ripples or bumps along the way. Et voilà! Dressed, not distressed.

In a rush? Spray tights with hairspray, which helps prevent (but does not guarantee) those running-out-the-door rips.

Got time? Freeze tights for 24 hours before wearing them for the first time. Run them under a tap, then place in a freezer bag and wait a day before defrosting. Returning the tights to room temperature helps reinforce the molecular structure of the nylon, thus making them more run-resistant.

HOW TO CARE FOR CASHMERE

"'I'm cashmere, for God's sake," it grumbles. "I deserve better than Rubbermaid.'"

CLARA PARKES, *THE YARN WHISPERER: MY UNEXPECTED LIFE IN KNITTING*

As fibres go, cashmere has serious pedigree and papers to prove it. Boasting a multi-tiered grading system, it operates an aristocratic caste even among its own kin. Grade 2, twill weave? Darling, make way for your Grade A, plain weave cousin, just 14 microns thick.

Harsh, perhaps – but that's why she's the grand dowager of natural fibres. Warm in winter, cool in summer, with soft downy hairs that demand an expert touch. She's no schlep. Much like any matriarch, she expects you'll understand how to care for her delicate constitution; and yes, she is rather precious (don't mention moths). But with proper care and attention, she'll leave you with a legacy of comfort and lived-in luxury which you'll cherish for years.

Washing:

- Turn inside out.
- Hand-wash the garment in a tub or sink of lukewarm water (hot water causes shrinking) using mild detergent (Woolite or dishwashing liquid), shampoo or, better still, conditioner.
- Perspiration odours? Martha Stewart recommends neutralising nasty niffs with ¾ cup of white vinegar.
- Soak the garment for ten minutes, swishing periodically in the water.
- Be gentle: don't wring, twist or rub the fabric. Think of it as washing a baby's hair.
- Drain the sink and refill with clean lukewarm water, taking care not to place the garment under a running tap (this causes stretching).
- Repeat the process to rinse out detergent.
- Gently squeeze the excess water through the garment.

Drying:

- Lay the garment on a bath towel (white prevents dye transfer) on a flat surface. Roll up like a sausage roll, pressing with your palms to remove moisture.

- Remove from the towel and smooth back into shape by squaring the hem and shoulders and placing sleeves parallel to the body. Flatten out pockets and button up buttons to avoid wrinkles.
- Allow to air-dry flat (hanging will distort the shape), keeping it away from direct heat and sunlight.

Maintaining:
- When dry, remove creases by ironing inside out on the wool or steam setting. Once again: be gentle.
- Remove pills with a razor (gently, of course) or de-bobbling comb. This improves the quality and softness of the delicate fibres. Think of it as combing a baby's hair.
- Give your garment some breathing space in between wears. More important, be careful what you wear it with. Avoid fabrics that will break down the fibres, like sequins that snag.

Storing:
- Once dry, fold your cashmere (never hang) with acid-free tissue paper. This protects the colour of the hair and preserves it from damp and dust.
- Store in a clean, well-aired, damp- and dust-free shelf or drawer away from natural sunlight.
- Line with rosemary- or lavender-scented sachets to discourage moths. Shake out on a regular basis, airing

briefly in sunlight to kill off any moth larvae. Some experts recommend freezing cashmere overnight (in a plastic bag), then defrosting slowly to kill any would-be critters.

- When storing away for a season, do not use cardboard boxes. Use a breathable sweater bag instead.

HOW TO WASH INTIMATES

Hand-washing is a dirty word, not least when it comes to caring for our unmentionables. The idea of tending to your smalls in the sink seems quaint, if not totally unnecessary. Surely a washing machine can do the job? Not so fast, modern gal! Tangling, chewing, bleeding and disintegrating are but a few verbs you can expect to use when extracting your knickers from a set of steel Bosch jaws. That is, of course, if you haven't already angered the ghost in the machine with a flimsy underwire offering, which it will chew and regurgitate with much in the way of hissing and spitting, not to mention a three-figure repair bill. The rule for intimates is simple: always hand-wash.

How to hand-wash:
- Fill a sink or tub with lukewarm water.
- Add one teaspoon of a gentle detergent or baby shampoo.
- Allow the lingerie to soak for up to 15 minutes.
- Gently rub the fabric to remove any stains.

- Rinse in cool water and lay lingerie flat between two towels.
- Press gently, taking care to blot out excess water.
- Reshape gently. Do not wring or manhandle!
- Dry over a clothes horse.
- If time, fate or fortune simply do not allow (e.g. fleet of children; crazy working hours; house renovations; in-law invasion), the following machine-wash alternative will ensure that your lacy bandeau and briefs don't look like they've been excavated from a medieval archaeological dig.

How to machine-wash:
- Separate lingerie according to fabric, natural from man-made. Synthetics attract the oils released from natural fabrics, which can, over time, create small spots or stains.
- Hook up bras (individually, not together) to prevent catching or tangling.
- Deposit underwear and bras in a lingerie bag according to fabric type.
- Wash separately. Do not mix with other clothing. Towels fill machines with lint that clings to lingerie fabrics; heavy materials tangle and stretch bras.
- Wash on a delicate or cold-water cycle.
- Reshape gently and line-dry. The heat from dryers destroys elastic and misshapes underwear.

HOW TO STORE A WEDDING DRESS

'I did get to keep the wedding dresses from *Runaway Bride*. They're all boxed up in my garage. I've never opened them. It'll be fun one day when Hazel is taller. She can play dress-up with her friends.'

JULIA ROBERTS

You paid a pretty penny for that cathedral-length Chantilly lace veil and Vera Wang silk sheath dress. It was worth it, though. You floated down the aisle like an ethereal vision. Only ten years later, it now looks as though you actually wore it on your hen night – stained, wrinkled and yellowing at the gills. *How much did you pay for it again?* Unless this was an intentionally postmodern Trash the Dress exercise, chances are you are mentally berating yourself for leaving it in the garage, sealed in a plastic bag, alongside the lawnmower, snow boots and kids' toys until you had a chance to find some proper storage space. Unless, like Pam Ewing, you can write off a pricey nightmare with *Dallas*-style 'it was only a dream' insurance (handy that), then it's best to utilise these hard and fast wedding dress storage tips.

Clean:

- Ensure that your dress, veil and other accoutrements have been professionally dry-cleaned.

Cover/package:

- Some dry cleaners offer a packaging service. If opting for this, insist the boxed garment remains unsealed to allow the material to breathe.
- Never ever hang a wedding dress in a plastic bag from the dry cleaners. See Chapter 8 for all the gory details – namely yellowing, mould and mildew. If hanging, use a 100% cotton garment bag or cotton bedsheet to protect the fabric from light, dust and moisture.
- Doing the packing yourself? Wear cotton gloves to avoid stains from skin oils.
- Use acid-free tissue paper to lightly stuff headpieces, shoulders and bust. This will help them retain their shape.
- Then lay the dress on a layer of tissue within the box. Be sure that there is tissue cushioning each fold. This will prevent heavy creasing.
- Store flat in a container such as an archival storage box that allows for the size of the garment – the fewer the folds and creases, the longer it will last.
- Garments that are left hanging can become misshapen from the stress on seams.

Store/preserve:

- Choose a dark, cool, dry space for storage. Avoid extreme temperatures in areas like attics, basements and garages. The ideal spot is an interior space away from exterior walls and pipes that might burst, and off the floor away from pets.

- Inspect your wedding treasures at least once per year. Look for any stains that may appear. You'll have better success the sooner the stains are caught. With clean hands (or gloves), fold items slightly differently, using the tissue to minimise creases and stress to fabric.

- Preservation should include protection from light, dust and insects, and the gown should never be wrapped in plastic – ever.

HOW TO PACK A SUITCASE

Getting away from it all does not mean taking it all with you. Unless you've got an imaginary Falcon 900EX on which to stow those Louis Vuitton luggage trunks (and a mini-entourage to carry them), you'll need to do a quick check-in with reality before checking in at the airport. That said, sometimes a bit of clever engineering is all that's required to get the maximum value from minimum space.

Before packing, lay out everything you'll need for the trip. Then follow the foolproof method below for maximising your suitcase space.

Bottom:
- Place heavy items at the bottom of the suitcase.
- Fit shoes heel-to-toe near the wheels of the suitcase. Stuff each shoe with socks and place inside a shower cap to keep soles from touching the clothes.
- Roll T-shirts, knits, jeans, cotton trousers and wrinkle-resistant clothes. Fold jeans in half and roll from hem to waistline. Fold in sleeves of knits and T-shirts and roll top down.
- Create extra room by placing in space-compressible plastic bags. This pushes excess air out of the clothes and minimises creases.

Middle:
- Fold delicate and wrinkle-prone items like shirts, dresses and blouses.
- Do likewise with jackets but turn these inside out first to help keep them smooth.

Top:
- Drape longer items like trousers and skirts which can be laid in layers the length of the bag.

- Line the sides of the bags and any nooks with smaller items like belts, scarves and underwear.
- Bringing a suit? Fold the suit from a hanger in a garment bag at the top of the case.
- Zip shut and check in. Happy travels!

HOW TO POSE FOR PHOTOGRAPHS

'To be natural is such a very difficult pose to keep up.'

OSCAR WILDE

It used to be that photos were only taken on special occasions: Christmas, school reunions, graduations and anything involving casseroles or several extended family members. This usually gave people a heads-up – enough time to plan an outfit and to get some extra grooming in place. Although you only had one shot to get it right, if it all went hideously wrong (squinty eyes, gaping mouth), there was a certain satisfaction in knowing the prints and negatives belonged to just the one person.

Now every micro-moment is a photo op. Going to the shops – take a selfie! Off to the pub – Instagram that round. Having a next-level row with your other half? Sharing is caring, kids. Despite the 2.0 convenience of fancy filters and thigh-gap apps (they exist!), the proliferation of amateur paparazzi means the bar has been raised. Learn how to strike a pose – you never know when the next camera will strike.

Body: Want to look slimmer? Always angle your body towards the camera. The only instances where this isn't permitted are mugshots and parodies of Grant Wood's *American Gothic*. Anything else requires standing to the side, shoulders back and stomach sucked in. Sitting? Cross the legs or roll your body weight slightly onto one thigh. Turn your hips away from the camera and place your shoulders forward, creating a slight twist in the body. Think Liz Taylor. She had it nailed.

Arms and legs: When it comes to creating shape, limbs are your secret weapon. Place both or either of your hands on your hips, holding your arms slightly away from the body. Then place your weight on the back leg, extending the front leg towards the camera. Sounds ridiculous but it works. When in doubt, look to pageant queens. Seriously, these gals know their stuff. Just don't wave.

Face: Rule of thumb: angles are your friend. Sweep your hair off the shoulder nearest the camera to open up your face. Elongate your neck and tilt your chin slightly towards the camera (this does away with double chins). Granted, you may feel self-conscious right now, so get in some practice, because it'll show if you don't loosen up. So lean your head a little to the side –

but not so far that you look like you've broken your neck. Need help? Practise in the mirror first.

Eyes: Nothing looks worse than two cigarette burns for eyes when the desired effect was a pair of sparkling windows to the soul. Top tip? Close your eyes and open them just before the photo is taken and say sayonara to squinting. Most of all, don't forget to 'smize' (© Tyra Banks) – smile with your eyes. Remember: you will blink and that's OK. What's not OK is barrelling wide-eyed down the camera lens. No points for the stalker stare. That's just weird.

Smile: Smiling is natural. Being told to smile while looking natural isn't. More often than not, grinning on cue betrays a sense of pain, fear or panic – sometimes all three. Smile widely and relax into a natural expression just before the photo is taken. If in doubt, try a closed-mouth or half-smile. Whatever you do, think happy thoughts. This is not a full frontal lobotomy; it's just a photo.

HOW TO SPEND MONEY ON CLOTHES

How much do you spend on clothes? More to the point, *how* do you spend money on clothes? Our wardrobes, over time, are one of the biggest investments we'll make, and yet also one of the least profitable and more troublesome to manage. Fast fashion and a flooded market have led shoppers to expect more for less, thus perpetuating an endless of cycle of buying and replenishing. Somewhere in every one of our wardrobes is a garment (or several) that simply isn't worth the acquisition price, regardless of what it says on the tag. Want to beat the market and avoid negative wardrobe equity? Then you have to know how and on what to spend your money. Prepare to open those closets to some insider trading.

Create a tailor-made portfolio: The key to establishing a well-balanced clothing portfolio is by aligning your financial situation with your personal goals. Spending any more than 5% of your monthly income on clothing poses a definite risk to your capital. The easiest way to determine proper asset allocation? If it doesn't reflect your current or projected needs, it's just not worth it. That's the bottom line.

Invest in high-yield pieces: Want to get the most bang for your hard-earned buck? Then split the difference between pieces that provide both short- and long-term yields. A mother of two may get more wear from jeans she dons daily, but she will get an equally great return from a classic wool coat and leather handbag that are worn less frequently but add to the overall strength of her investment portfolio.

Spread the risk: Diversification is key to a well-maintained portfolio, so shop around. Look at dividing your spend among different asset classes – designer, mid-range, trend-led and less expensive pieces. Spend the least on trends and invest in quality cuts and fabrics (the best your money can buy) that'll go the distance.

Be mindful of the overall portfolio: Consider the Aristotelian proverb 'the whole is greater than the sum of its parts.' In other words, don't get tempted by an individual item unless it can add to and improve the functionality of your closet as a whole. You will simply wind up paying more money in the long run to buy pieces which justify its presence.

Look for a return on investment: Worried about parting with too much cash? Think of the future performance of what you buy. Although designer pieces don't always warrant the inflated price tag, some do have a competitive return on investment. Luxury labels like Chanel, Prada and Hermès keep a consistent resale value over time, as opposed to of-the-moment brands whose value is more dependent on market fluctuations (what's hot, what's not). What does this mean for you? Items that retain their value are bona fide assets and will fetch a decent resale price at auction, in consignment stores and on vintage resale websites.

HOW TO SPOT A FAKE DESIGNER BAG

The words 'discount' and 'luxury' tend to be mutually exclusive. Rarely seen in company together, luxury prefers to rub shoulders with a select few, protecting her exclusive reputation with a hefty price tag – especially when it comes to designer handbags. Recently, though, crafty con artists have been sneaking behind the velvet rope, copying mannerisms and convincing others of their pedigree, all the while making a few (billion) bucks off someone else's name. Although most designer brands have their own authentication processes, there are certain criteria that apply when buying serious arm candy. Here's how not to fall foul of the phonies.

Use the front door: Everyone loves a bargain but often if the price is too good to be true (€3,500 marked down to €350), that's generally because it is. The time you spend scouring the internet for deals could be better spent buying from the designer or a reputable department store. In doubt? Always revert to the company's official website for a list of official vendors. Also, bear in mind that certain fashion houses like Hermès, Chanel and Louis Vuitton never discount. So if it's hot, you'll most definitely get burned.

Dodgy accents: Hardware like zippers, closures and clasps are a dead giveaway. First off, they should all have the same colour and finish (with the exception of Chloé, which uses mixed hardware). More exclusive brands prefer precious metals that are heavier to the touch. If the metal accents look light, flimsy or likely to tarnish – you've got a dud on your hands. Likewise, zippers should always open and close seamlessly without bumps or snags. Some labels also use embossed styles or ones that are set up to lock and hold. It's these nuances that make certain bag styles trickier to copy.

A stitch in time: Shabby stitching is the true hallmark of a huckster. This is not to be confused with hand-stitching, which, although not perfectly straight, is frequently used on high-end bags. The difference? Stitches shouldn't be frayed, misshapen or sloppy. As for seams – these are rarely glued. Would you put glue near exotic leather? Exactly.

Look inside: Counterfeit bags can trick the eye from the outside but open it up and you'll discover a few tell-tale signs. Cheaply attached lining, crooked inside labels and bogus authenticity cards give the game away. Fraudsters have even mimicked date codes, serial tags and hologram stickers, so don't be fooled. Always do your research.

Leather: Ah, the fresh smell of glue, rubber, chemicals (delete as appropriate)! Doesn't have quite the same olfactory audacity as leather, eh? If it claims to be real leather, then it should smell and feel accordingly. Rub your hand across the bag – is the texture soft but dry? Good, then you've got the real deal. Anything that feels a bit sticky or oily is plastic in disguise. If it looks a bit shiny after a few wears (especially the handles, which should start to soften), then congrats, you've got yourself a dud.

The devil is in the detail: Bent on a bargain? Always look to legitimate retailers like The Outnet, TheRealReal, Yoox, Blue Fly and Gilt and to end-of-season sales on respected retailers' websites with a reputation for authentication. Unfamiliar websites offering discounted limited stock merchandise and sham sites bearing names similar to that of a designer are red flags. Conversely, any site selling multiples of exclusive bag styles is also most definitely bogus. And don't be fooled by a 'Made in Italy' or 'Based in London' reassurance. Rogue traders often set up a shell company to facilitate the distribution and sale of goods made elsewhere – often in China. If the 'Contact Us' section only offers an email address or a country code 86 (China), you've got your answer.

HOW TO CRACK A DRESS CODE

'Dressing is the one art the unqualified must practise.'

ELIZABETH BOWEN

Dress codes. They're not what they used to be. Ever since flexible terms like 'business casual' and 'wow wear' have infiltrated the dress code lexicon, most of us poor sods have been set adrift on its semantic raft. Will a football jersey fly in the boardroom? What if nobody is wowed by what I wear? What then? Such confusion is not only a social peril but one that could warrant a P45 should Dress Down Friday at the bank be translated as mini-skirt and belly-top. There'll be a dressing down alright – just not what you may have expected. Need a translator? Why didn't you just say so?

Casual: Misleadingly simple, Casual gives the impression that anything goes but secretly hopes you turn up in printed leggings and a boob tube so that unmitigated judgement can be had. Best bet? Err on the side of caution by cross-referencing the venue, time of day and general vibe of the event in question. A picnic in the park with friends will allow more leniency than a corporate picnic with colleagues. If in doubt, ask yourself if what you're wearing will potentially have you arrested, fired or socially blacklisted. Then set fire to those Daisy Dukes.

AKA Come as You Are (just don't)

Smart Casual: Smart Casual stresses everyone out with her double-barrelled presence. Why? No one is quite sure what to make of her. Does she mean a skirt and blouse or a skirt and T-shirt? Will she give me those 'should have known better' eyes if I turn up in flip-flops? Propriety is a big deal for Smart Casual (even if she pretends she's oh-so-relaxed), so avoid any fashion faux pas by leaning more towards the 'smart' end of things. If you get her seal of approval – just act casual.

AKA Style Limbo

Business Casual: Blame the Obamas. Ever since Michelle met the Queen in a cardigan and Barak ditched the tie and jacket for weekend White House wear, there's been some radical style politics afoot. To suit or not to suit? Bare arm or sleeves? Flats or heels? It's Friday, now what? The unending questions. As if climbing the corporate ladder wasn't challenging enough. Rule of thumb? No jacket required, but neither is anything you'd wear to a festival, beach, gym, bed, nightclub or someone else's bed. There. Sorted.

AKA Obama Casual, Dress Down Friday

Work Wear: Different industries have different dress rules. Even so, there's a prevailing sentiment regardless of whether you work as an accountant or a graphic designer: don't allow what you wear to overshadow what you have to offer. The clothes may not maketh the woman but when it comes to the office, they certainly provide some non-verbal clues. What is your plunging neckline really saying? Would you do business with a floral sundress? I rest my case.

AKA Business Standard

> I arrived at a 'new grad' group interview for a blue-chip company shortly after I finished university. I was confident about my chances. After all, I had two shiny degrees and a 'can do' attitude. Sitting among the sea of navy suits, I silently congratulated myself at thinking outside the box and choosing not to go corporate. This was my chance to shine – only I interpreted 'shine' as 'Mae West does Wall Street'. The interview didn't last long. My fur-collared cardigan, viscose camisole and metallic fleck trousers did all the talking, sadly, and brought a shock of diffuser-dried curls and fuchsia lipstick along for the gab. I didn't get the job.

Cocktail Attire: If Cocktail Attire were a long drink she'd be a Cosmopolitan – colourful, classy and lovely to look at. Even so, she doesn't take herself too seriously; she's not Black Tie, after all. When combining drink and a dress, be mindful of the golden rule: show leg or boob – never both. No one wants to start the night looking like that girl who's had one too many.

AKA Semi-formal

Creative Black Tie: Any invitation that says 'creative' should be approached with caution. Combine it with 'black tie' and we've got a sartorial landmine underfoot. Aping anything worn to the Met Ball may not translate to terra firma. Aim instead for one standout accent – an unusual colour, tactile fabric or interesting piece of jewellery – and pare everything else back. Do not confuse a formal occasion with clown school.

AKA Festive Wear, Wow Wear, Dress to Impress

I received an invitation to a party in Paris with a 'Wow Wear' dress code. Curious as to what that entailed, I did a quick Google search and came up with several entries for TLC's infamous *Toddlers and Tiaras* programme. Seemingly a pageant byword for fancy, Wow Wear is apt to entail: a flipper (fake teeth), a glitzy cowboy hat and a frou-frou frock. I decided to split the difference and opt for a pink beaded vintage dress. My bad. I arrived to a sea of black – jeans, T-shirts, blazers, vertiginous boots – and not a sequin in sight, not one, nada. I was literally in the dark. Don't Parisians do dress codes? Where's the respect for protocol? It was then that the proverbial penny dropped (surprising that I even spotted it). Style semantics are rather flexible and need to be cross-referenced culturally as well as literally. 'Noir', I discovered, is French for 'wow'. Who knew?

Black Tie: Although still a bit blurry around the edges, this one is easier to pin down than its Creative cousin. Aim for a long dress (not necessarily a formal gown) or a fancier cocktail number. Just avoid anything too short and whatever you do, lose the platform shoes. Single soles are much more refined and less likely to incur an untimely speed wobble. If in doubt, ask 'What would Grace Kelly do?'

AKA Formal

White Tie: Off to a state dinner? Check you out! This is grade-A Cinderella territory here which requires suitable regalia – namely, a ballgown and white opera gloves. Tiara optional. Seriously ...

AKA Fancy Schmancy

HOW TO CREATE A HAPPY CLOSET – BALANCING WELL-BEING WITH BEING WELL-DRESSED

'Happiness is the place between too much and too little.'

ANONYMOUS

Discover your closet type.

Before decluttering your closet, declutter your mind.

Identity the emotional drivers and pay-off behind your shopping habits.

Target and isolate your shopping triggers.

Ditch the excuses.

Put limitations on choice.

Find your signature style.

Create a uniform of interchangeable staples with a top layer of moveable trends.

Upgrade your relationship with clothes.

Learn from the past – just don't take it with you.

Live in the present but understand that the self evolves.

Accept who you are now but watch who you become.

Get to know yourself and your image through the eyes of others.

Let the outside reflect the inside.

Remove what no longer serves the person you are today.

Face up to procrastination. What you resist persists.

Treat your closet to regular check-ups.

Curate your space with the right tools, techniques and technology.

Allow for space – don't fill it.

Feel the flow.

FURTHER READING

Baumeister, Roy F. and Matthew T. Gailliot. 'The Physiology of Willpower: Linking Blood Glucose to Self-Control.' *Personality and Social Psychology Review* 11.4 (November 2007).

Clear, James. *Transform Your Habits: Learn How Psychology Makes It Easier for You to Live Healthy and Actually Stick to Your Goals.* jamesclear.com, 2013.

Dean, Jeremy. *Making Habits, Breaking Habits: How to Make Changes that Stick.* Oneworld Publications, 2013.

Dobelli, Rolf. *The Art of Thinking Clearly.* Sceptre, 2013.

Duggan, Leann. 'The Dead Giveaways that a Designer Bag is Fake – or the Real Deal.' Refinery29 (www.refinery29.com/how-to-spot-a-fake#page-3), 2014.

Duhigg, Charles. *The Power of Habit: Why We Do What We Do and How to Change.* William Heinemann, 2012.

Fiore, Neil A. *The Now Habit: A Strategic Program for Overcoming Procrastination and Enjoying Guilt-Free Play.* Revised ed. Penguin, 2007.

Graves, Philip. *Consumer.ology: The Truth about Consumers and the Psychology of Shopping.* Revised ed. Nicholas Brealey Publishing, 2013.

Gurfein, Laura. 'Here's How to Spot the Difference Between Real and Fake Designer Bags.' New York Racked (http://ny.racked.com/2015/3/10/8182935/fake-handbags), 2015.

Kondo, Marie. *The Life-Changing Magic of Tidying: A Simple, Effective Way to Banish Clutter Forever.* Vermilion, 2014.

McGonigal, Kelly. *Maximum Willpower: How to Master the Science of Self-Control*. Macmillan, 2012.

McLeod, S. A. 'Cognitive Dissonance.' SimplyPsychology.org (http://www.simplypsychology.org/cognitive-dissonance.html), 2014.

Mischel, Walter. *The Marshmallow Test: Understanding Self-control and How to Master it*. Bantam Press, 2014.

Nechita, Gabriel. 'Who is Winning at the Game of Marketing? Email vs Social Media Stats.' Padicode (http://padicode.com/blog/web-marketing-2/email-vs-social-media-statistics/), 2014.

Peck, Joann and Suzanne B. Shu. 'The Effect of Mere Touch on Perceived Ownership.' *Journal of Consumer Research* 36 (October 2009).

Ridley, Jane. 'Killer Heels: Christian Louboutin, Jimmy Choo Knock-offs Rip Off Buyers, Prey on Child Workers.' *New York Daily News* (http://www.nydailynews.com/life-style/fashion/killer-heels-christian-louboutin-jimmy-choo-knock-offs-rip-buyers-prey-child-workers-article-1.430625), 15 July 2009.

Salkovskis, Paul and Sinead Lambe. 'We are All Hoarders but for Some it Spirals Out of Control.' TheConversation.com (http://theconversation.com/we-are-all-hoarders-but-for-some-it-spirals-out-of-control-35967), 2015.

Schwartz, Barry. *The Paradox of Choice: Why More is Less*. HarperCollins, 2004.

Underhill, Paco. *Why We Buy: The Science of Shopping*. Simon & Schuster, 1999.

Yarrow, Kit. *Decoding the New Consumer Mind: How and Why We Shop and Buy*. Jossey-Bass, 2014.

WEBSITES

ApartmentTherapy.com
HangerProject.com
MarthaStewart.com
TheSweetHome.com